Praise for Sherry's Blog

Great idea to lighten up and just ENJOY the great years we have left. Your writing is very beautiful, moving and true! You are a good spokesperson for our age group.

Alice Shechter

Thanks for your blog! Funny! Honest! Inspiring! I recognized myself at every turn!

Paulette Barrett

I am enjoying your blogs so much – they are real, heartfelt, very sweet and thought-provoking.

Talia Schenkel, Ph.D.

Your descriptive writing is a pleasure to read.

Eric Stotter

Terrific! I always enjoy your wonderful reflections.

Madeline Naegle, Ph.D.

Your essays totally resonate and make me laugh because they are so true!

Susan Hein

NOT DONE YET
The Humor of Aging

Sherry Deren

Mediacs Books

New Paltz, New York

*Mediacs*Books
36 Henry W. Dubois Drive, #8
New Paltz, New York 12561

Editor: Carol Bergman
Cover Design and Interior Drawings: Juliana Suárez-Lipton

Ordering Information:
Quantity sales. Special discounts are available on quantity purchases by corporations, associations, and others. For details, contact the "Special Sales Department" at the address above.

Not Done Yet: The Humor of Aging/ Sherry Deren
ISBN 979-8-9894765-2-7

For all of us seniors who are not

done yet. We all have much to do—

to enjoy and to contribute to

others—for as long as we have.

And for my large, extended family

TABLE OF CONTENTS

PREFACE

I started writing humorous personal essays soon after I retired from my career as a research scientist in 2019. Although writing was what I did for most of my work life, scientific writing generally does not include humor, unless it is the topic of study. Researchers are trained to be objective when presenting their research designs and findings, and avoid the personal "I."

My career spanned more than 40 years. Toward the end of that time, I began thinking about what I wanted to do next. As I got older, I kept feeling surprised that I was becoming a senior; it was something that I just never thought would happen to me. And although I saw the whole thing as a joke played on me, I knew things were changing; I was viewing some things from the perspective of an aging person, and I noticed that sometimes people responded to me like I was an older person. That surprised me too. Eventually, I began to appreciate some of the changes I experienced related to aging, and even welcomed them.

I had always enjoyed writing, and I found that, as I wrote, I could easily see the humorous side of getting older. And writing from the first-person perspective encouraged me to be honest about what I was experiencing. Within six months of retiring, I started a blog. This book is a compilation of entries from the first four years, including the Covid-19 years. And though Covid is a backdrop to many of these essays, I am hoping that by the time you read this book, the pandemic will no longer be a vivid memory. That said, it is also, in a way, a document of a recently retired person during the pandemic, and beyond.

NEW CHALLENGES

MAINTENANCE

As I struggled to stay in the "plank" position for one full minute, I thought: why am I doing something so uncomfortable? After I finished and collapsed onto the mat, I raised that question with my trainer. "For maintenance, that's why. I am proud of you and often use you as an example," he said. I appreciate my trainer's pride in me. However, being complimented for maintaining a plank for a full minute did not seem to be on the same level of achievement as some of my previous accomplishments as a research scientist.

Throughout my life I have been one of the lucky ones. I haven't needed to give much thought to what I had to do to stay healthy. Over the past 20 years, though, I have noticed some changes: my weight has slowly increased, gray hairs have slowly appeared, and my memory for names has (more rapidly) declined.

The media is filled with advice for the increasing number of seniors in the population, and the buzzword recommendation in the United States for this population is "maintenance." I used to think of "maintenance" as a kind of homeostasis, meaning something that remains stable or constant. Not anymore. I now believe that it is about slowing down decline in multiple arenas, including physical health, appearance, and mental acuity. I find this definition more motivating for taking action. I also have another incentive: I looked at some recent photos taken at family gatherings and wondered why my older sister had gotten so thin, until I realized that she wasn't the one who changed! So, I decided to embrace maintenance in several ways:

First, I make monthly visits to the hair salon to get my gray roots colored dark brown. It does the job, but costs time and money, and since I recently retired, I am less concerned about looking older than many of the folks still in my office. Or am I? Furthermore, while the hair dye can make my roots brown, the ongoing thinning of my hair still gives away the fact that aging is going on up there. I have already learned to do some artful positioning of the remaining hair to reduce scalp exposure. Does this constitute high maintenance? More about hair dye in my later essay, "To Dye or Not to Dye." It is an important subject!

Second, I attend to my mental capacity. Various types of exercises like crossword puzzles and Scrabble have been promoted for the aging population, and I enjoy them. But research indicates that skills learned while doing these puzzles and games don't transfer to improvements in general memory or other brain activities. Given the oft-cited mind-body connection, I hope that my health club activities also help in the maintenance of my cognitive abilities, sort of a 2-for-1 deal.

But most of the recommendations I read about are for physical health, with exercise as a major component. So, third, I joined a health club, where I concentrate on cardio and strength building. In my twice-weekly visits, I do cardio on the bike for about 20 minutes and then meet with the trainer for stretching, core and other types of strength-building exercises, or, as he calls them "resistance training." (I have come to understand the source of the resistance—me!) I often do these with an exercise partner, my 85-year-old neighbor. Unfortunately, she has started having memory problems and I usually need to call her several times before our exercise dates to remind her about them. When I do, she is eager to go.

It's often fun doing exercises together, except for two parts of our exercise routine: when the trainer tells us to toss a ball back and forth to each other, or when he asks us to stand on one leg, alternating legs, for a minute or two. I know that these are for coordination and balance, which are important for folks my age to reduce the chances or consequences of falling. But I feel like a child and am embarrassed doing them. They certainly aren't the exercises my trainer does; he has bulging arm muscles and a well-defined "six-pack." And the buff 30-somethings around me in the gym are lifting enormous weights and doing one-handed push-ups. In any case, because of my shoulder arthritis and rotator cuff problems, I probably shouldn't lift heavy weights. I am okay not even trying those.

I have recently added another weekly visit to the gym because upcoming family events will likely generate photo opportunities. I will continue playing Scrabble just because I like it (brain benefits or not), and have found that expanding my reading and exploration of cultural activities (and writing a blog!) are all fun and mentally challenging. And I will continue to enjoy the visits of my granddaughter, who loves to go outdoors with me, play catch, and compete to see who can stand on one leg for the longest time. Somehow, with her, I enjoy it and I never feel embarrassed.

STAGES OF CHANGE FOR MY CHANGING STAGES

I conducted behavioral research related to substance abuse for many years, and became familiar with a construct called the "Stages of Change Model," developed by Prochaska and DiClemente. This model posits that individuals may move through five stages as they undertake health behavior change: **precontemplation, contemplation, preparation, action, and maintenance**. Clinical and research efforts using this model strive to identify someone's stage, and work to encourage movement to the next stage. For example, someone who uses drugs heavily may not initially be thinking about reducing or stopping drug use, and is therefore in "pre-contemplation." However, if this person goes to a counselor to discuss problems at work, the sessions may reveal that drug use plays a significant role in the individual's job problems, and the counselor may encourage the person to consider reducing (or stopping) their drug use and move to "contemplation." Through planning and discussion, the client may begin to prepare for making changes and then undertake actions to reduce use. In the—sometimes—final step, the client is able to maintain a lowered drug use or abstinence behaviors.

Although there is a logical order to these stages, it has been recognized that movement is not unidirectional, and individuals may return to earlier stages during their change process.

I think that these stages of change also apply to adapting to the process of aging, as follows:

I was in **precontemplation** about aging for many years before actually accepting that I was officially an older person. I didn't retire until my 70s, and my life after retirement became busy with many new activities and social events. It took about a year and I was in **contemplation** about how to manage this new stage of my life. I'm not sure exactly when that happened—but the combination of my chronological age, acceptance of senior citizen discounts, graying hair, and enjoying my membership in the senior network in my apartment complex—all played a role.

I began thinking about what my aging meant. And that brought me to the **preparation** stage. Now that I had fewer externally imposed deadlines and responsibilities, and the motivation and ability to choose what I wanted to do, what did I want my life to be? I knew I wanted to write more, so I joined a writer's workshop; my desire to explore the city's sites and see family and friends meant I needed to make specific plans and schedule dates and activities. Once I had the general plan outlined it was easy to move to the **action** stage. Yes, there are some weeks that I am not as active as I'd planned to be, and I go back to **contemplation** and revise some of my plans. I soon move again to **preparation** and then get back to **action.**

I now consider myself to be in **maintenance.** I make time most weeks to read, write, see friends, and visit something new. And these activities are rewarding and reinforcing.

I believe the "Stages of Change Model" will remain helpful in the future. The life phase I am in now will change in the coming years. My level of energy may substantially decline, there may be limits on my mobility, family responsibilities may emerge, or I may even need to depend on others. I am in precontemplation about all of these. But I hope to modify my activities as my life phases change, and to reach desirable maintenance levels for each new phase.

DESIGNER SENSES

I experienced a decline in hearing while I was still working, and made necessary adjustments, like sitting closer to the speakers at seminars so I could hear them. After all, I thought, hearing aids were for old people, not me. But when I began having difficulty hearing my 12-year-old granddaughter and often had to ask her to repeat something, I decided to get my hearing checked.

When the audiologist tested me, I learned that the ability to hear high frequency sounds, like my granddaughter's voice, is especially likely to decline with age. I laughed when she said that more people come to her about hearing problems with their grandchildren than about difficulties hearing their spouse. I think this may not just be due to the differences in the pitch of their voices!

I now have two hearing aids and my hearing has definitely improved. I put them on in the morning right after I come out of the shower and dress. But I have started thinking that there should be designer features on them that could be adjusted by the wearer, given advances in technology. For example, I have a friend who is very sensitive to other people's voices and empathetic to their moods. While this means she can instantly sense painful feelings, and helps make her a wonderful friend, I wonder if it might give her some rest if she could turn off—or even turn down—that capability on her hearing aids.

Similarly, wouldn't it be nice if we could increase the volume on the hearing aid when something complementary is said to us—even adding appropriate music. And best of all, if only we could mute the sound when anger or criticism is expressed.

And what about designer features for vision aids? Last year I had cataract surgery, replacing my lenses. My vision has improved, but I still see reality. Most of the time this is what I want to look at, but not always. It would be nice to have bionic lenses that allowed me to adjust what I see. Reality would be my usual setting, but sometimes I would like to block out the sight of messy garbage on the street, or to enhance a setting with brighter sunshine. Also, if I was talking with someone who was somewhat over-bearing in the advice they were giving me, perhaps I could reduce their influence by temporarily making their face fill with ugly pock marks and scars. This would divert my attention, making it more possible for me to question, or even ignore, what they were saying.

Dentistry could also develop designer features. With aging comes teeth replacement, including implants, bridges and dentures. This could open a whole world of tasty possibilities. What if some teeth replacements came with salt and pepper options, or other favorite condiments, like sage or marjoram, or even ketchup and mayo. We could just tap the appropriate tooth, and the food additive would appear as we chewed. I guess we'd periodically need to get refills, but what a time saver this would be, and it might encourage the exploration of new food tastes. Clearly, mouthwash should be an option in this redesign.

So, what's the point of these designer senses? I propose that as we age and need replacements or fixes for some of our equipment, rather than simply looking to restore the previous functioning of our senses, there should be efforts to enhance and improve on the capabilities that have declined.

That makes the most sense to me.

TO DYE OR NOT TO DYE

I started dyeing my hair about 20 years ago. I have very dark brown curly hair, and when gray appeared it was quite obvious. My mother, who had a similar hair color and texture, had very little gray up to her death at eighty-five. Given our many physical similarities, I thought my hair would also remain dark throughout my life. When gray started coming in, it was clear that would not be so.

Art by : Juliana Suárez-Lipton

Until my 40s I never spent much effort, time, or money on anti-aging remedies: no special face creams, cosmetic surgery, or hair coloring. The idea of growing old gracefully appealed to me, especially since I never imagined that I would become an older woman. But when I saw the gray coming in, I felt that it made me look prematurely older. I started having my hair dyed.

This continued throughout my professional working life. As my career advanced, many of my colleagues were younger than me. I felt it was important that I continue to dye my hair so as not to be seen as older. I planned to stop once I retired. My resolution lasted about eight weeks into my retirement. Once I saw substantial gray coming in, I reverted to hair-dyeing.

I realized the truth of something a friend said years ago. Her husband once told her, "You don't have to keep dyeing your hair for me." Her response was that she wasn't doing it for him. I too was no longer doing it for colleagues; this was something for me.

Within a year of my retirement Covid restrictions shuttered hair salons. I considered this an opportunity to see what my natural hair would look like, thinking I could now age gracefully. I didn't like it.

A friend reported doing an informal survey of the women she knew, asking what would be the first thing they would do when the Covid restrictions were lifted and shops reopened. The most frequent response was to go to a hair salon to get their hair cut and colored! We both laughed at that. But not for long.

As my gray hair took over more territory, I felt older whenever I looked into a mirror. My hair salon opened about three months into the Covid shutdown period—and without too much wavering—I was back to hair dyeing.

But now there's another concern.

My hair is thinning and I wondered if hair dyeing was exacerbating the problem. Would I have to choose between more gray hairs (if I stopped dyeing) or fewer but dark hairs?

My hairdresser tried to reassure me and said she recently changed to a hair color product that used natural ingredients that would be good for my scalp. I looked up the ingredients: sugar and rice milk ! I'm not sure if sugar and rice milk can actually reduce hair loss, although they sound yummy for a pudding. Still, the "natural" hair dye gave me some hope that the thinning problem might improve.

My hairdresser reported that several of her clients had recently talked about hair loss and were told by doctors that it is stress-related, brought on by the pandemic. Since I had recently received my second vaccine shot, my fears of getting Covid had declined. Maybe my hair loss would also decline. This has become an ongoing discussion with my hairdresser. One day, when I told her I was upset by the hairs I saw every day on my white-tiled bathroom floor she had a suggestion: "Change your tiles to a darker color." Was she joking? I'm not sure. For now, I will continue dyeing my hair and I don't plan to change the tiles in my bathroom. After all, I think I always knew that dyeing was inevitable.

MORE OR LESS CHANGES IN MY BODY

More Growths

I used to be proud of my skin. Somewhat dark complexioned, as a teenager I loved lying in the sun during the summer and getting tanned. I had a few dark moles on my body that my mother called beauty marks. I never minded them. Anything I had called "beauty" was fine with me. Fast forward about 50 years, and my body started having many add-ons; some even look like what used to be called beauty marks. But according to my husband, they are called tags. TAGS! Like something found on an object in a yard sale and sold "as is."

More Skin

I was never overweight. Okay, maybe a little. But still, where did all that extra skin on my arms and thighs and face come from? I never could have filled in all that space. And who would have thought that gravity, an abstract concept, would play such a significant role in how I look.

More Weight

Talking about weight, who ever said, what goes up must come down? Weight loss plans work for my husband, but not for me. Between ups and downs, ups are far ahead.

More Comfortable Clothes

While all these changes are taking place, I have also found that comfort in clothes is more important to me. So no more high heels—except for very special occasions—and no need for tight-fitting clothes or short skirts that keep me from crossing my legs when sitting down. And now, thanks to pandemic lockdowns, I have learned to appreciate elasticized waistlines; no one can see them on Zoom calls.

Less Hair

I always had thick, dark curly hair, typical of my eastern European Jewish heritage. It was so curly that as a pre-teen I had what was called a "poodle" cut, and in my 20s, in line with the fashion, it became an Afro. Now it is thinning, as I have already mentioned. My kindly hairdresser tells me that it was too bushy before, so now it is an improvement, but I know better. Sometimes less is not more.

Less Energy

I used to have three young children at home, a full-time job, and a long commute to work. Life was busy, but I had the energy for it all. Now retired, living in New York City, and with just my husband at home, I anticipated that my energy would be used for extensive day-long explorations of the city. It hasn't turned out that way. Pre-Covid when the city was open, I found I had less energy than I expected, and midday naps were sometimes needed.

Less Acuity of Senses

Vision and hearing have been declining for several years. Thankfully, unlike energy loss, there are tools to help restore them: glasses, hearing aids, cataract surgery, etc. Perhaps the results will make these senses better than ever, and I can move this item from the less to the more category.

Less Multitasking

I remember days when I would push my body to exhaustion. With children and a job, there were numerous activities to be done outside of work, sometimes two or more simultaneously, like walking the dog, helping children with homework, preparing a paper or presentation needed for work, making meals, shopping, and many more. Now, I often plan a more leisurely day, including scheduling time for relaxing.

So, if you ask me how I am managing the aging process, I will say: overall it's not bad. Most days I feel pretty good—more or less.

Downsize-UPSIZE

I have associated the word downsizing with life changes, like a reduction in the number of employees in a business or moving to a smaller home. Both seemed like actions that could lead to reduced costs and greater efficiencies. But the benefits are not always so clear.

Several years ago I moved from a four-bedroom suburban home to a two-bedroom apartment in the city, giving up a finished basement, a formal dining room and a large backyard. The move involved considerable downsizing.

But I traded my larger home living space for the sites and conveniences and activities that Manhattan had to offer. I definitely saw it as up-sizing.

I also gained about two hours every day of commuting on a bus. Definitely upsizing there too.

As I age, I am finding more up/downsizing happening in my life. Some don't involve much of a change, but for others, the outcome has been mixed.

Getting shorter is a literal experience of down-sizing. I was surprised recently when my doctor told me I was 5'2". I had lost over two inches from my adult height. But I don't mind: it makes my grand-children seem even more mature and older when they are next to me. Also, I had always liked having a husband who was just a few inches taller than me, and this difference has remained; he has lost about three inches too.

I recently gave up a parking space I paid for in my building, and am selling my car. Neither my husband nor I drive anymore, and there are lots of public transportation services available in Manhattan, including buses, taxis and other ride-hailing services. We have mixed feelings about giving up our car; it provided some sense of independence and freedom. But we no longer have the expenses of parking and car insurance. I'm not sure if this is upsizing or down-sizing.

And what about the memory losses that are a normal part of aging? Is this loss another aspect of downsizing? We recently bought my husband a new computer, upsizing from 4GB to 16GB of memory. At first I thought it would be great if I could also quadruple the memory in my brain. Then maybe I could remember everything. But while remembering all the joyous times would be wonderful, being able to forget past hurts and angers can be comforting and reduce stress. This is one example of upsizing that requires careful selection: what to leave behind, and what to take with me.

My retirement from work several years ago involved downsizing, and initially reduced my daily sense of accomplishment and purpose. But having time for other activities I enjoy such as volunteer work with immigrants, has been an extensive and positive upsizing. But being more at home during Covid times led to some personal upsizing—in my weight! That's one area where I want to change direction and will be downsizing for sure. So what have I learned from sizing up (ouch! sorry) these changes? Size doesn't matter. I am likely to experience expansions and reductions throughout my life, and this will apply to many things, including my possessions, activities, and weight. But taking charge of what is happening, to influence the direction and its contents, is the challenge.

MAKING REALLY "NEW" RELATIONSHIPS

I have been thinking about the psychological concept of transference. It occurs when feelings or attitudes toward one person are applied (transferred) to someone else. This may occur in psychotherapy, when patients transfer feelings they had toward a parent or other significant person from childhood, onto their therapist. It is believed to occur unconsciously, and can be a useful tool for the therapist in working with the patient. But it also happens to most of us in everyday life.

I thought of it recently when I visited my niece in Florida. On two occasions I called her Dara, my daughter's name. I think this occurred because I love them both, feel very at ease with them both, and the emotions I feel for my daughter were simply transferred to my niece.

I laughed when I called my niece's dog the name of my grandson! Both are warm and loving, fun to be with, great to hug, and shorter than me. Perhaps as I get older, some emotional boundaries are coming down, and emotions that I feel towards more than one person—or even a pet—may spill over, and get transferred between them.

I think I also experience transference when contemplating baby names. When a friend or relative talks to me about choosing baby names, I sometimes have strong, visceral reactions to certain names. Some of my feelings are readily understood since they are tied to current figures in the news or famous people who I either like or don't like. But some reactions loop back to people I knew in elementary school who I had not thought of in decades, but whose names raise either strong positive or negative feelings. How strange that emotions about people I knew a long time ago emerge in situations that have nothing to do with them.

Transference also occurs in relationships with partners. It is believed that some people choose partners because of their similarities to—or differences from—someone significant in their childhood, usually a parent. This can lead to the attraction we feel for a partner as well as how we relate to them. The transfer of feelings and attitudes developed from one person to another one later in life can have positive or negative consequences for the relationship. And we may not even know why we are having the reactions to them that have emerged.

I have been thinking about some people I met in recent years. I felt shy with a new neighbor who was a tall imposing woman. I think she reminded me of a 1st grade teacher I had who I was always a bit afraid of. I was reluctant to become more friendly with this neighbor, and may have missed the opportunity for a good relationship.

When a new CEO came to head an agency I worked for a few years ago, I believed he was competent and would help the agency grow. This led me to share concerns I had about senior staff members and the agency's operations. It soon became clear that he had little interest in making changes in the agency and even resented my suggestions. My misunderstanding about his intentions interfered with the quality of our working relationship. The transference in that situation was from my father. He always seemed a fair person, benevolent and wanting things to go well at home. It would have been better had I waited a while longer before deciding to share my concerns with the new CEO.

Then I realized that the longer you live the more significant relationships you have. Does this mean that as we age, there is some transference of emotions and attitudes from prior relationships, especially our primary ones, to most new people we meet? Does it get harder to respond to someone purely based on who they are, and not who they may remind you of, often unconsciously. Is it possible to halt this unconscious reaction to appreciate the uniqueness of the person who reminds us of someone else? Not surprisingly, the other person may be experiencing transference also. When we meet, the room may be crowded with unseen people that we both have brought with us, some not even alive anymore. I try to keep these uninvited guests quiet and in the background, but it's not always possible. As we age and accumulate more relationships, there are more of them.

*   *   *

AS GOOD AS IT GETS

I am beginning to understand a change that is occurring as I age, related to how I feel about my health status. When I was younger and felt sick or had a health problem, I went to my doctor, was treated, and was cured. Afterwards, I felt as though I had returned to my prior state of general good health. Sometimes I didn't even need any health care, just a few days of rest and I was "good as new."

But as I get older, there have been changes in my overall health status— new muscle aches, periodic memory lapses, and lowered energy—things that will not be cured. I have learned that they are not serious or life-threatening conditions, but just part of getting older. I can reduce the impact of some of these changes, like taking ibuprofen for muscle aches, keeping a note pad handy to jot down things

I want to make sure to remember, or planning rest times in-between activities likely to make me tired. Reversal of these conditions is not likely, but with a healthy diet and regular exercise, I hope I can slow down the speed of decline.

And for certain health conditions that often emerge with aging—like knee or hip pains, skin growths or tumors, declines in hearing— there are multiple successful treatment options, like knee replacements, Mohs' surgery, and hearing aids. Some of them require periodic doctors' visits and tests to determine if conditions are worsening. I realize that I will never again be "good as new," nor ever again free of thinking about some of these health concerns. Perhaps the biggest change for me is the realization that I am vulnerable to many of the conditions that always belonged to older people I knew, and I thought did not apply to me.

I have entered a new era of how I perceive my health status. I have some chronic and emerging health issues and concerns, none serious. For the most part they have stabilized, primarily with the aid of treatments, and some require periodic doctors' visits for monitoring. A friend told me of someone who never goes to the doctor, her motto being "don't go, don't know." That's not the route I want to take. When a health concern emerges, I seek out medical opinions as to the best treatments. I don't like spending time in doctors' offices or undergoing imaging procedures, but I go when it is recommended.

And I conclude that there is little to be gained from bemoaning the loss of a state that probably never was. Changes in health status and needs occur throughout life, with more conditions to be addressed as I age. I am basically healthy, and am fortunate to have no serious genetic diseases (that I know of). Most importantly, I have lots to do in the years ahead. And though I may never again be "good as new," maybe that is really not so desirable as it implies a loss of all I have learned and accomplished over the years. I will take care of my health so that for each stage of my life I can keep it "as good as it gets."

UNDER NEW MANAGEMENT

ACHES & PAINS

As I finished my physical therapy session for my lower back, I asked my therapist, Fran, if this problem would be cured in a few more sessions and how long I would need to continue the exercises she had taught me. "The problem doesn't really go away, you just learn to manage it," she said.

I felt as if this was one of those aha moments, the kind when you realize that you have had an insight that would have a profound change on how you see things.

I had arrived at a new realization. When I was younger, I always felt that all the health issues that I had could be cured or at least diminished to the point where they were inconsequential to my everyday activities. Now I was beginning to realize that there would be health-related issues that required life-long management.

I carefully got off the PT table. I managed the periodic pain from my torn rotator cuff—it could not be repaired—with careful body movements. I then had to sit down to put on the enormous black boot that my podiatrist had prescribed earlier that week, for the tendonitis in my right leg that was making it difficult for me to walk. He said I needed to wear it for about one month. I also put on the splint on my left thumb, that I had been wearing for about two weeks to reduce the pain from my trigger thumb. This would shortly be relieved by a steroid injection, and I learned that wearing the splint probably just made it worse. But at least this problem was quickly resolved. Walking out to the street to return to work—I had not yet retired at the time—I took out my distance vision glasses, as I was looking for a place to buy lunch. The store lettering down the block was a bit fuzzy. I had been told that I would need cataract surgery soon.

What has become of me? I asked myself. I was now the kind of person I always knew existed and saw around me, people with back, leg, vision and other impairments.

I know I should be grateful. I do not have, as I write, any acute or life-threatening condition. But I realize that many of the changes in my body can never be cured or reversed; I'll be visiting doctors and therapists more frequently. And I have to learn to accept this.

MANAGING DOCTORS

For most of my life the doctors I saw were older than me, and it seemed that was how it should be. I believed that their age brought experience and wisdom. When I noticed that the pediatricians who took care of my children were my age, that seemed fine too. Their youth meant they might be better able to relate to my children, and since they weren't that long out of medical school, their knowledge was likely to be up to date.

Once I got into my 40s, some of my own doctors were suddenly younger than me. And as I have gotten older, much to my surprise, others have even retired. How could they do that? I thought they would always be there for me. This generational shift got me thinking about some things:

How should I address my much younger doctor? I am generally informal with people I meet and don't use titles. However, doctors usually address me using my first name, but I don't know if I should call my doctor "Dr. X" or use his/her first name. Doctors are probably trained to introduce themselves with their title to give patients confidence in them. Starting with "Hi, I'm Harvey" may not elicit confidence in some patients. However, since I am now older than most of them, and am a doctor too (a PhD), it seems strange not to use first names when we address each other.

How can I get their best medical advice? In a recent visit to a doctor, we discussed whether I needed to undergo an optional medical procedure; I asked for his opinion. He said, "If you were my mother, I would say you should..." Even though our age differential made it possible that I *could* be his mother, I wished he had said, "If you were my wife," or even "sister." Then I realized that what was more important was whether he actually liked the person he referred to, be it his mother, wife or sister, and would do his best to keep them healthy.

But could I ask him what he would recommend for someone in his family he really liked? Perhaps next time.

How do doctors view me? In a recent visit to a new doctor, he looked down at my chart and said, "You look 10 years younger than your age." I know he meant that as a compliment, but, trust me reader, ten years younger than my age is not too young. I feel—and thought I looked—at least 20 years younger than my age. Perhaps training for doctors should include something on this topic in a module called, "Developing Rapport with your Patient."

How can I manage the increased frequency of medical care visits? Taking care of myself now requires more doctor visits and medical services. Nothing serious, but increases in bodily aches and pains, and changes in hearing and vision, involve referrals to medical specialties and services—like rheumatology, orthopedics, and audiology—that I always thought were for older people. I guess I qualify. The amount of time these visits require surprises me, and it would be a challenge if I were still working full time. Still, I have other things I'd rather do.

How can I adjust to these changes? These are my ideas: I will appreciate the fact that my doctors' youth means they have more current medical knowledge, and I will not call them by their first names until there have been several visits and we are both comfortable using first names. I will assume that they love their moms, so that I will welcome advice preceded by, "If you were my mother... ." And, unless there is an urgent medical problem, I will manage multiple medical appointments by scheduling them around the things I want to do. Finally, I will make staying healthy a priority, so I don't have to think too much about any of these things.

WORRY NOT

I have always been a worrier. I have worried about important things, like the illness of a family member, a critical project at work, or concern about a teenager being out too late. Worry or stress has been shown to be useful, and can signal danger, or the need to act, so I am fine with worrying about those kinds of things. But, like most people, I have engaged in many hours of absolutely useless worrying about unimportant things.

Research has shown that as people get older, they are more satisfied with their lives. I hope that a reduction in worrying will be part of the improvement in life that I experience as a retired person.

To help me further my worry-reduction efforts, I looked back on my worrying career and analyzed my experience of useless worrying. I found that this worrying had several sequential stages: anticipatory, early stage, intermediate, full-blown and relief. I will illustrate with two examples of worrying about unimportant things: what to wear at an upcoming professional conference and what to serve at a family birthday dinner party.

In my work as a research scientist, I attended many conferences, and as the matriarch of a family with six grown children, most partnered, there are a lot of celebrations.

Anticipatory Worrying

The event is still far off, six months or more. It feels like worry is nibbling at the edges of my consciousness, mostly in the background, and, therefore, no sleep is lost.

I'm scheduled to present at a conference. Where should I buy the dress or suit? And what about my weight? I would like to lose some weight before I go shopping.

Then there's the dinner party I am planning. First, I gather a list of guests and their particular food needs. Our family has vegetarians, pescatarians, vegans, and gluten-free folks. I'm not too worried about omnivores. Lucky for me there are some omnivores.

Early Stage of Worry

The event is now three-four months away. Specific items to worry about are emerging. Early "to do" lists are made so I can be sure to worry about all relevant elements. Plenty of time remains, and still no sleep is lost.

A quick check in my closet reveals nothing I want to wear, so I need to go shopping. Some earnest worry begins, and since I now have a plan to lose weight, I don't want to buy something that won't fit well... so I put off shopping.

I have the guest list for the dinner party, but should I cook or ask people to bring things? Cater?

Have it in my home or in a restaurant? Lots of items to fret about.

Intermediate Stage of Worry

The events are about two months away, and free-floating worry has begun, sort of an angst that I wake up with every day. Some sleep is now lost. I go to a shop and start trying on things, but since there's time, I don't have to get something yet, and nothing looks quite right. Also, I am still trying to lose weight.

I need to make final decisions about whether to cater, cook or go out. The guest list is finalized. Since the event is a happy occasion, I try to enjoy this planning. But what gift should I get? Ah, another item for the to-do list.

Full-Blown Worry

The events are now about one month away, and substantial sleep is being lost. I have entered the acute stage of worrying. I do more shopping, and at last, I buy something that may or may not need alterations. I experience some relief. But what about a purse, shoes, jewelry? I can ratchet up the worrying again, but now I have only a few weeks left, so I rush to get everything else I need.

Decisions about food have been made for the party. But something unexpected may happen at this stage, for example learning that some out-of-towners have decided to attend. Where will they sleep? How long will they stay and do I need to make plans for them? Also, some of the guests may not get along. Will they make it uncomfortable for others?

Relief at Last

This usually comes on the eve of the event since there's not much left in terms of decisions to make. It lasts through the event period. All goes well.

The clothes for the conference were laid out and the speech finalized the night before the event. I am ready. My talk is well-received, attendees ask me questions and want a copy of my paper.

As for the dinner party, arrangements are done, plans are set, and there is nothing more to do the night before. The dinner goes well and guests happily take home leftovers.

At this point it would appear that worrying is over, but it isn't.

Regrets

Once an event has passed, I should be able to stop worrying. Not so. Regrets about conferences, speeches, and parties have worried me months and even years after the event. There was an event where I gave an excellent presentation, but in pictures of the event I thought the suit I wore didn't look well on me. I still think about that. And I remember a dinner party where I had loads of shrimp, and I forgot to put out one of the shrimp dipping sauces. This was decades ago, and it still bothers me. I can't call this worry, just useless regret, a different kind of "leftover" from events.

Cumulative Lifetime Worry

I estimate that overall, I have engaged in worry at least three days a week, for an average of 30 minutes daily, although some episodes have lasted through substantial parts of the night. Some of this worry time was significant and legitimate. But most of my worry time was for unimportant things, adding up to years of my life. What I could have done with that time!

Worry Space Available

I have discovered that after some worries dissipate, there is always space available for new ones, so that the overall quantity of worry does not decrease. For example, if I was worried about an upcoming event, after it is over there is some breathing room created, but soon the space operates like a vacuum, searching for and sucking up a new worry. That's quite amazing. If they could invent an air balloon with this feature, you would never need to worry about it getting punctured, losing air and descending, as a new influx of air would immediately fill all the available space.

So, what's to be done to reduce useless worrying?

I have some ideas:

1. I will accept the fact that I will never be worry-free. In small doses, for appropriate purposes, worry is helpful. I will use it to signal me to take needed actions.

2. I will allow myself, in the midst of the acute stage, to seek symptom relief (candy bars and alcohol for me), but only in moderation. I will still deal with the concerns.

3. I will think about what I could accomplish and enjoy if some of that worry time was used to do things I like and be with people I care about.

4. I will reduce stress by following the guidelines many health organizations have published on

stress reduction methods such as exercise and relaxation techniques.

5. I will not worry about any of this. I have started retirement with many interests and activities: traveling, writing, socializing. All of these are serving to reduce my worry space. Furthermore, in retirement, I do not have to attend any conferences and my children now invite us to their dinner parties. Yay to that. Worry not.

MANAGING TIME

During my 40 year+ career, I was always task-oriented, whether there was a project at work to finish, or household chores to do. Time seemed very limited. There were always multiple tasks waiting to be done, so I worked hard to get each one completed as best and as quickly as I could. Now that I have been retired for over two years, I see that my "get it done" philosophy is starting to wane.

While this change serves to reduce daily stress and the pressures of working under constant deadlines, I am finding that I don't like it. When I was working I readily postponed certain activities because there was no time for them. Now I simply postpone them. I do many worthwhile activities that I didn't have much time for when I was working—reading a book for pleasure, visiting a museum, calling a friend or family member, watching a movie—but what about those things I had on my to-do lists for all those years that I now have time for? They are still getting postponed and my postponement strategies seem to be growing. Here are some examples:

1. Cleaning out my closets: I know there are things there I don't wear anymore. They could be donated and become useful and enjoyable to others.

2. Going through my file cabinets: There are papers that I have kept to "look at later," to decide if they are worth keeping. Later has arrived and I still don't know what to do with those accumulated papers.

3. Registering for and taking a Spanish conversation class. I always wanted to improve my Spanish, and shortly after retirement I enrolled in a conversational Spanish class and enjoyed it.

The class ended with Covid lockdown, but I still haven't enrolled in another course.

4. Calling some people that I "should" talk with, including family and friends. Maybe I don't really want to speak with them, and postponement of this is not just because of a shortage of time.

5. Writing essays on a regular basis. Although I write for my monthly writers' workshop, I postpone doing it until shortly before class each month.

6. Starting and sticking to a serious diet. There are some popular intermittent fasting diets—eat five days and starve for two, or eat eight hours in a day and starve for 16. These sound feasible, but I get stopped by the starving part, so am putting this off too.

Strategies I use to postpone and what I tell myself:

1. I'm ready to do a task but I realize I haven't eaten for a while, therefore it's time for a snack.

2. I just finished creating my to-do list for the week. It seems overwhelming and I need a break.

3. I'll do just one more game of "Words with Friends."

4. I should turn on the news and see if anything important is happening.

5. Wow, look at my nails. I didn't notice those cracks. Before I start anything I should file them down a bit. Some nail polish would look nice, too.

6. I'm tired... maybe a little nap, and then I will jump right in.

7. I haven't been out of the house yet today... I'll just go for a little walk.

8. Writing more regularly. I can't think of anything to write about right now... maybe later.

9. And as for going on that diet, maybe I will start about two months before that big wedding. That should be a long enough time.

I have learned two main lessons from my postponement strategies: First, I need to look at my commitment to the item being postponed. If I feel no commitment to it and it's not urgent, then I need to either cross it off the list of things I should do or put it on my "long-term delay" list. Second, If I still have a commitment to the task, just do it!

* * *

DON'T SAVE THE BEST FOR LAST

I have an idea for a new New Year's resolution: Don't save the best for last. This has been a habit of mine I want to change. But first, some examples:

1. At meals I often save the best for last. If I cut up my steak and there's a particularly juicy-looking piece, I put it aside, and eat the rest first. When having a fruit salad, I eat the smaller and less appealing pieces first, and then the luscious piece of strawberry or melon at the end.

2. When I read the newspaper, if there are several articles I want to read, I leave the one I am most interested in for last. I read what I think I should be up to date on first—about the latest political wrangle, or latest atrocity in a part of the world that's far away. And then I read the story about a politician or issue I have strong feelings—positive and negative—about. This is followed by the op-ed page, as I begin eagerly

anticipating the daily crossword puzzle. I save that for last, after my reading is completed.

3. In Covid time, when my trips outside of the house became less frequent, I did the smaller household tasks first, and left the outside trips that I enjoy more—food shopping or bus rides to visit a friend or museum—for later in the day.

4. I have a few friends I enjoy talking with. When I plan to call them, usually in the evening, I wait until I finish cleaning up after dinner or looking through the mail. Why do I do this? Maybe I enjoy the anticipation of something to look forward to, so I extend the anticipatory time by delaying having what is most desirable. Also, in terms of tasks, if I get the little things out of the way, then I have the rest of the time for the ones I enjoy more, and I believe I can do them with no time limitation.

I admire others who act differently. They start their meal with the best piece of a dish, they look briefly at the front page of the newspaper and go directly to what really interests them, and they do the tasks they care most about first, leaving the less desirable ones for later.

I now find that saving the best for last may no longer be the best strategy for me. When I get to the end of the meal, I may feel full, and not enjoy that tasty morsel as much as I had anticipated. After reading all the parts of the paper that I think I should be informed about, sometimes I feel so depressed and hopeless that my energy has declined and I skip the puzzle. And when I put off tasks I am most interested in doing, whether it's a trip outside of my home or a call with a beloved friend—I sometimes find that I have run out of energy—and don't do it. My resolution is that I will change my ways and go for the most pleasurable first. Why not? Perhaps the best can be now— and it is up to me to choose to make it that way.

Don't Get Stuck At Your Setpoints

Our bodies have setpoints. These are stable and optimal ranges of some physiological characteristics, like our weight and even our experience of happiness.

Research indicates that genetics accounts for about 50% of setpoints, so that means we have some control over the remaining 50%. I have had mixed success trying to nudge my setpoints.

In my late teens through early 30s, I stabilized at a certain weight, regardless of what I ate. After giving birth to two children in my 30s, my setpoint moved upward, and remained constant for many years. As I approached retirement, reductions in metabolism and too many retirement parties and cocktail hours contributed to weight gain. I remember a friend's advice about life, "If you don't let yourself go, you will never know how far you can get." It made sense to me at the time, and sounded liberating, but I learned that this is not a good way to manage weight; post-retirement, I am under new management.

I wish weight were like a thermostat, and I could just move a dial down a bit and the desired change would happen. And why is it easier to achieve a higher set point than a lower one? It doesn't seem fair. Lowering this setpoint requires effort.

My sense of happiness setpoint is one that I would like to move up. There has been some debate as to whether this can be modified over time. Some research has shown that when you experience a major event, like winning a lottery or losing a spouse, there may be a temporary change in the experience of happiness, but it's only temporary. Others say there can be long-term changes after these events.

Sometimes, when I wake up in the morning, I feel worried and uneasy. I have found that simply hoping or waiting to feel happier never works. But getting into action and doing things I enjoy can override my feelings. I may need to remind myself of this on some mornings, but it definitely works for me.

Other setpoints I have thought about include how I experience negative emotions, like frustration or anger. I have different setpoints for these emotions, with the feelings occurring more readily than my willingness to express them. As I get older, this discrepancy has become more disturbing to me. Simple things like someone rudely getting ahead of me in the super-market line can set off anger, and in the past, I would try and ignore it rather than addressing it. I have come to the conclusion that I don't need to be shy about these feelings anymore. If I express my annoyance, politely and directly, I find that the feelings are more quickly dissipated.

So, I am adjusting my set point dials in these two areas: feelings and expressing them.

I also have set points for behaviors, like my level of activity and engagement in life. When I was younger, with a full-time job and young children, I rarely thought about my activity setpoint; I simply did what was the urgent priority. I often felt "used up" by the end of the day, and this seemed good and purposeful. Now my children have their own lives, I am retired, and I have more choice about what to do with my time. But at the end of some days, I feel incomplete, and I think it's because my setpoint was based on my level of activity when I was younger and had more responsibilities. I need to adjust this setpoint so that I can enjoy not feeling exhausted at the end of the day.

So, what have I learned about my setpoints? While they are part of who I am, I think that in new life phases, new levels may be desirable and attainable.

To Do and Not To Do Lists

When I had a full-time job and children at home, I prepared multiple "To Do" lists. The lists were long; they included necessary tasks related to family, work and friends. Each week I made new lists and prioritized items in the lists, most of which got done, eventually.

Now that I have retired, I still organize my week by making lists, but they are quite different. Most of the items are not necessary, they are there because I want them to be there, I choose them to be there. Even more satisfying: I don't usually have a deadline.

Some items resemble my old "To Do" lists, like shopping for food, inviting family for dinner, or calling a friend who is ill. But some of the new items have never been listed before. I also have started a "Not To Do" list.

At the end of the week I often find that I have enjoyed what I have not done almost as much as what I have done. Here are examples of my new lists, of things to do or not to do, every week.

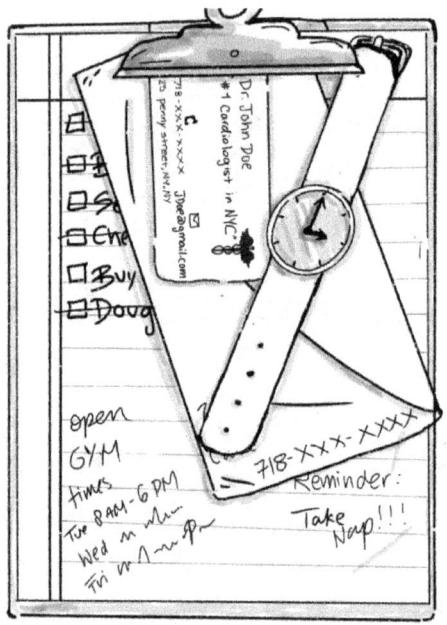

1. Do something at home just for pleasure that you haven't done in the past, such as going back to bed after breakfast or spending the entire day reading.

2. Call someone you lost touch with, someone who you always cared about, but didn't have the time to contact. Make a phone date to have a lengthy conversation.

3. Acknowledge someone by expressing appreciation or really thanking them. For example, tell a close family member or friend that you love them or enjoy being with them. Or thank a stranger, someone you just meet doing errands. Tell them you like their smile or appreciate their service, and watch their face afterwards.

4. Visit a place in your neighborhood that you have passed through before but never really "seen." It can be a store, park, or just a street corner. Spend a few minutes there and observe what is going on.

5. Do something by yourself that will give you a sense of accomplishment, like going to the gym or visiting a museum you are interested in, or even cleaning out a drawer. Yes, even cleaning out a drawer.

Not To Do

1. Don't shower and dress as soon as you wake up in the morning. You don't have to go to the office for a meeting. Remember, you can relax.

2. Don't do the dishes right after dinner; they can wait.

3. Don't wear clothes that feel uncomfortable when you are home. Pants with elastic waists can be a great source of pleasure.

4. If you have started reading a book and you find that it doesn't engage you, don't read it anymore. Give it to someone else or discard it.

5. Don't get the mail as soon as you know it has been delivered, and don't open the bills until you are ready. But don't wait too long to put this on your "To Do" list.

6. Don't answer the phone as soon as it starts ringing, especially if you are in the midst of doing something. Chances are it's one of those robocalls. If it's important, the person will leave a message. If you are enjoying what you are doing, turn off your phone.

I wish I had discovered "Not To Do" lists earlier in life, it would have helped me focus more on what I think is important. Both kinds of lists can be helpful and enjoyable.

* * *

MANAGING SUCCESSFUL AGING

I have always been achievement oriented. As a child I worked hard to get good grades. As an adult I tried to be successful in the many roles I had – student, parent, wife, research scientist, friend, and others. Perhaps that's why when I heard about the concept of "successful aging" it appealed to me. Now that I am fully along in the aging category, I certainly want to make a success of it.

But what is success in aging? It seems to me that it's one of the few things that you shouldn't have to work hard at to be a success... just keep living. No need to cram late at night like I did for school grades, or write research proposals like I did to be a successful research scientist, or make sure my children had their homework done as I needed to do as a parent. I just need to wake up in the morning, and know that if I make it through the day, I had another day of successfully aging.

But wait—there has been a lot written about successful aging, so there must be more to it than that. Maybe I can learn something to help me be even more successful. Looking through some of the writings on this topic, I found a book on *Successful Aging* by Rowe and Kahn. Three components were described:

1. Absence of Disease and Disability

I agree with that. So far I am successful in this component, although doctors' visits and medical tests seem to be taking more of my time. But I can keep up with preventive health care.

2. High Cognitive and Physical Functioning

"High" is relative, but I do a lot of reading, some writing, and can discuss the terrible state of the country with knowledge of the latest outrageous headlines. In terms of physical functioning, I exercise almost every day (ok, maybe 3-4 days/week), and go for long walks several days each week (ok, once or twice).

So far, I'm a big success. That wasn't hard.

3. Active Engagement in Life

I think this is a big one, and for me it is my main source of pleasure. During Covid, it was challenging, though. Visiting family and friends was replaced by Zoom or Facetime calls. Trips to explore other countries or parts of the US were reduced to local bus travel to shop for necessities. Enjoying live theater, museums and other entertainment morphed into Netflix, television, and online shows.

Does this mean I am a failure in this component of successful aging? No! I have redefined engagement in life as something I can do from my desk chair, when necessary. So I declare I am successful in this last item too.

But wait—success should also be sustainable. What will happen as I continue to age? My cognitive and physical functioning may decline, as may my engagement in life, especially since it is somewhat dependent on my health and functioning. Am I prepared?

Also, since people close to me who I love are getting older too, if they need my assistance I want to help take care of them. This no doubt will reduce the time I can spend on some of those activities that have made me successful in aging so far.

But maybe providing this care for aging others can also be part of successful aging, and while my activities are likely to change over time, I can still find many that are meaningful to me. But I think I will also hold on to my initial idea—that simply being here, every day, and looking forward to a new day doing things I enjoy, will mean that I am mastering successful aging.

LEARNING TO PRIORITIZE

I needed to call the telephone company, buy a carton of milk, return a friend's telephone call, and pay a bill. What happened to the day? I accomplished several items on my To Do list, yet there was a feeling of dissatisfaction.

I remember taking a course on time management and the trainer used some props: a fish tank, a large boulder, and many smaller rocks, or pebbles.

The trainer started by putting the pebbles in the tank, one by one, and showed that once they got to a certain level, there was no room to fit the boulder. He then emptied the tank, put in the boulder first, and slowly added pebbles one by one. It was easy to see that many pebbles would easily fit around the boulder.

I enrolled in this training to enhance my management skills at work, and this demonstration made clear that if you saw the tank as the time you had in the day at work, you would accomplish the most if you started with the big items, and didn't use up the space with little ones. The training was successful. I learned that if I had a big task looming, like a grant proposal, or a research paper, I should tackle that first at the start of the day, and then as the day proceeded I could fit in the smaller items, like returning a phone call, reviewing a colleague's research concept paper, meeting with my administrative staff, etc. If I started with all the small items, I would run out of time for what was most important to me.

When I retired, I looked forward to having ample time for my various interests. But I didn't. I soon realized that I can use my time management training at this stage of my life. I have identified some boulders that I am eager to have in my life, including writing blogs and other essays, reading books for pleasure that I never had time to do, and exploring museums and neighborhoods. Although Covid brought some limitations to the city exploration task, there were many places that could be explored using face masks and following social-distancing protocols. I adapted and kept going. But when I started out my day with the boulders, pebbles often get in the way. These were not trivial tasks, and included things like food shopping and paying bills; each seemed like it could get done in a short time period. But there were always several of these every day, and together they filled up a big part of my fish tank. And then there was no room for my boulders.

Now I have a new approach and it seems to be working: At the beginning of each week I plan my boulders, generally in three or four-hour blocks of time, for at least three days during the week. These boulders are the first activity for that assigned day, unless there is an urgent pebble or medium-sized rock to be taken care of. I also designate some time each day for pebbles, both planned (like bill-paying) and unplanned (an unexpected phone call). If I am in the middle of a boulder I may pass on the unexpected pebble. But if it's something I know I will enjoy, like a chance to have coffee with a cherished friend, I will do it and come back to the boulder as soon as I can.

That's the plan. So far it is working and I have space for boulders, pebbles and unanticipated activities.

Napping and Other Health
Lessons from Childhood

I always thought that taking naps was something only little children needed. It usually occurred twice a day until they were about two years old, then once a day until they were four or five. It gave the parents a break, and the child often awakened less cranky than they were before taking the nap.

It was only after I retired from full-time work that I began appreciating the pleasures of a brief nap. "Power napping," defined as a mid-day nap of about 20-30 minutes, has been associated with many benefits, including increased energy and better memory. While I worked full-time and especially when I was raising children, I never had the time to take naps. On days that I felt tired, I simply pushed through and did what was needed. But now, if I feel tired in the middle of the day, sometimes I take a brief nap. I love it, and I too am less cranky after waking, ready for engagement in whatever I planned for the rest of the day.

So I started wondering if there are other behaviors associated with early childhood that may be useful to my health now.

My mother and Bubba (grandmother), both of whom raised me, always extolled the benefits of getting me and my siblings out of the apartment to have fresh air, even if temperatures were below freezing. This is a good idea for me now. I find that when I am working at home all day, even at something I enjoy doing, if I haven't been outdoors, I feel a little dejected by the end of the day. Checking on some research, it has shown that fresh air increases your intake of oxygen, improves circulation, lowers your heart rate, and has other benefits. And there's another benefit: going out reminds me that there is a big world out there with many sources of stimulation and pleasure. So I plan to go out more often, perhaps after I wake from my naps.

Other behaviors associated with childhood that are good for me may require effort to do successfully. As a child, if I fell and hurt myself, I wanted an adult to take care of it. Getting concrete help, like the application of a little iodine or mercurochrome on the wound, and a bandage, was important. But even more important was knowing that there was someone who I could go to if I was hurt who wanted to help me get better. That's still important now. I can usually figure out the concrete steps to take if there is a physical wound. But for emotional pain I have learned that going to a close friend or relative, someone who listens and cares when life's challenges seem hard for me, is needed for healing.

I have concluded that many of my childhood behaviors have been forgotten or replaced by activities more appropriate for my age. But I will continue to look back to find those that can still serve me, as wisdom comes from many sources.

Relaxing Can Take Work

When I retired, I thought that I would have more time to relax, and it would be effortless. That hasn't been true. Because of the busy life I had, with work often extending outside of regular office hours, when I tried to relax it felt as if I was wasting time, that I wasn't being productive.

So I looked up the word relax. Most definitions include words like less tense, calmer, and rest. That sounds about right, in terms of what I want to achieve, yet I find it hard to get there.

First, if I just sit in a comfortable chair and put my feet up, I am flooded with thoughts about tasks I need to do, even if they are relatively simple like taking out the garbage, making a phone call, or buying milk. I keep a pad and pen near me when I want to relax so I can write down the tasks that come to mind. I learned this from the Erhard Seminar Training (EST) that I took in the 1980s. They gave advice about how to get a good night's rest if there are things you need to do the next day that are worrying you—just write them down on a pad, and let the pad worry about them overnight. That has been helpful in terms of helping me fall asleep, but when I want to relax, I keep thinking of new undone tasks. The other problem is that while I am in my comfy chair, if I feel tired, I fall asleep. I don't want to do that because then I will miss the pleasurable sensation of relaxing and if I sleep too long it may interfere with my sleep at bedtime.

There are plenty of suggestions out there about how to relax, including things like taking slow deep breaths and doing mindfulness meditation. I have done these, but only for brief time periods; perhaps that's why when they end I don't feel much more relaxed. Other advice recommends certain activities, like doing yoga, getting a massage, or taking a bubble bath. But these are not very appealing to me, as they involve some preparation or planning, and getting up, and I usually want to stay in my chair.

Of course there are some old standbys that are not healthy, like drinking alcohol or smoking (weed or regular cigarettes). Although I have tried these to relax, for general health reasons, I want to limit their use.

So what's to be done? I think I have found what may work for me. I checked the etymology of the word relax and learned that it comes from the prefix *re* — meaning to go back, and *lax* – meaning to loosen. In other words, it means to return to a state of less tension, which means that a state of tension /activity/accomplishment existed after the last period of relaxation and is needed before the currently sought after relaxing period can begin. This means I need to plan for a period of activity that will give me a sense of accomplishment and a little tension before I can relax again. Since I usually have many tasks on my To Do list— like making the needed phone call to the cable company, or ordering the new pillows for my bed, or even writing that next essay—there is no lack of activities. And after I complete a task and am satisfied with what I have done, I should be able to comfortably settle into the chair and relax. It will be almost as if I have earned the time for relaxation. But wait—unfortunately, sometimes undertaking and even completing a task may not be satisfying, it may in fact increase tension. I may need to undertake two or three of them before I am ready to *relax.* Hopefully there is still time left in the day.

Hmmm, this may not be as easy as I thought. It looks like relaxing may take some work.

SOME PLEASURES OF AGING

THE TIME OF MY LIFE

As a logophile, a person who loves words, I often enjoy thinking about words or expressions with multiple meanings. There are some expressions that change in meaning as I get older. *The time of my life* is a phrase that I think a lot about now. I am in *the time of my life* when I can look back on phases that are completed, and am fortunate that I can make choices in doing things I like. But the other meaning of the phrase, as conveyed in *having the time of my life,* has become more important to me: I want to enjoy myself. It's my time and my time to enjoy myself.

Another expression that has evolved in meaning for me is *free time.* When I was younger and busy with work and children, having *free time* was scarce. When I did have free time, I relaxed with my family. Now I realize that my *free time* is not actually free, it is spent when I use it, and its availability diminishes.

I'll do it later is a phrase with multiple meanings, especially the "later" part. And I think there are gender differences. When I decide to do something later, if it's a household task (like doing dishes) I usually do it within the hour. If it's calling back a friend it might be within a day or two, but if it's cleaning out a closet—it's usually within a month, or maybe months later.

When I ask my husband to do some household task—like throw out garbage, make the bed, *etc.*—and he says, "Okay, I'll do it later," I have learned that this is not likely to be within the next hour; it may be any time later that day or even the next day, in which case the request to make the bed becomes moot.

I had a girlfriend who enjoyed herself on a blind date that ended with her date's declaration: "I will call you later." After a year had passed with no efforts at contact, I guess he really meant much much later, or maybe never.

Let's meet for a coffee is another sentence that has changed over time. When I was working, it usually meant having coffee or tea to discuss some office or work matter. These days, it has little to do with drinking coffee. It might mean: *Let's meet, I have a problem to discuss,* or, *we haven't seen each other in a while, let's get together and reconnect.* Since I rarely drink coffee or tea anymore, for me it means an opportunity to see a friend, and likely we will have a bowl of soup, or an alcoholic beverage. We rarely have coffee.

When setting a time to meet with a friend I often tell them I can meet but *not too late.* When I was younger, *not too late* meant I could meet them until about 10 p.m., and if we couldn't get together in person but wanted to talk, it meant that they could call before midnight, my usual bedtime. Now when I make arrangements with others, *not too late* means we can meet no later than 7 or 8 p.m., and they can call until 10 p.m. It's not that I am asleep by then, I just know I am less able to provide the level of attention that I'd like to have.

So, what do these changes in the meanings of words and expressions signify? Most of them indicate that I am becoming more aware of time and how I use it. And I need to keep in mind that having *the time of my life* is always my goal.

ID CARDS

My passport and driver's license are my most frequently used documents to prove my identity, generally used for things like checking in at the airport or cashing a check. I went to a New York Mets game recently at Citi Field, and when I bought a beer, I was asked for an ID card as proof of age. I smiled as I looked for my driver's license. And so did the older woman who sold me the beer. I think it is policy to require proof of age for anyone buying alcohol at certain athletic events, to reduce potential disagreements with those who may not look old enough. But it seemed a waste of time.

On the other hand, when I took an Amtrak train a couple of years ago, and requested the senior rate, I was asked for an ID to prove I was old enough to qualify. I enjoyed that request. It seemed a fine use of my time.

I have other ID cards with photos that I use to get benefits I am entitled to. I have a New York City

Senior Citizen Metro Card that allows me to take buses or trains at half fare. That's great. And I have an EasyPay account, which means my metro card is tied to a credit card, so that when the balance gets below $10, it is automatically replenished. This means I don't have to wait in lines to refill my card. Nice.

But the card has another benefit. It has an expiration date, and I am automatically sent a new replacement card every two years. I have often wondered if anyone checks whether or not I am still alive, and still living in New York City, but I am happy to get it, as it involves no effort on my part. And the newly issued card uses the same photo I submitted when I first applied for the card, more than ten years ago. I appear to have been a little plumper in the face than I am now, but otherwise it's just a younger version of me. And I have a card issued by the apartment complex I live in; it gives me access to enter my building. When new cards were issued several years ago, they used the same picture I took when I first moved in, more than 15 years ago. My hair is no longer that color, but so what? Whenever I use these ID cards, I feel my age has been fixed at an earlier time in my life. I don't mind that.

I also have other ID cards that are no longer of any use, but I keep them as documents of my past. These include the ID card issued by New York University during my career as a research scientist there, and the one I had when I was a New York City cab driver during my graduate school days. The most cherished one is the ID I was issued when I worked at Two World Trade Center; I was there until 9/11/01.

I will keep all of these cards even though they no longer generate benefits other than memories of my history, and of 9/11, a day that I was fortunate to survive.

MEMORIES

Memory loss is a natural part of aging, and for most people it starts in the 50s. When I think of happy or pleasurable times in the past, whether with family, friends, or at work, I feel suffused with warmth and a sense of gratitude. Being able to talk about the memories with those who were present when the events occurred is an additional source of pleasure, but I can still enjoy them even if the others who were participants remember nothing.

Many wonderful memories were created with my husband and children. We went on cruises together and had many family get-togethers, but it's some snippets of events that have stayed with me most clearly. Like the time when my son was in preschool, at four years old, and was in a Christmas play. I don't remember the name of the show or even the plot, but I remember him on the stage wearing a red and blue snowsuit and hat. He was using a little broom to symbolically and purposefully sweep away the little girls dressed as snowflakes in white sparkling tutus who were also on the stage. It is as though it happened last month, not almost 40 years ago. And it has been seared and sealed into my memory, forever. My son doesn't remember.

My sister has Alzheimer's disease. When I last visited her a few months ago, we spent some time together mostly speaking Yiddish, the language we both learned as children, when our Bubba (grandmother) lived with us. We talked about many things, including our parents, our children and the weather. I was careful to never mention her current situation, her plans, or the recent death of her husband of 60 plus years, which she doesn't remember. She had some formal schooling in Yiddish and I never did and we laughed a lot as I struggled to make myself understood and she corrected me. After I left, I called to let her know I was home. "When will you come visit me?" she asked. My sadness about this was quickly replaced by the pleasure we both had when we were together, and I savored the time as I recalled our conversation. But she remembered nothing.

I recently went to see my 18 month old grandson. He lives four hours away, so visits are not very frequent. We spent an afternoon together alone, as his parents were working. We played with many toys, including a big bag of Lego blocks that to my surprise he noisily turned upside down to empty, and then put them all back in, one by one. When he finished, he kicked his feet up and down while sitting on the floor, loudly repeating, "Yay." He was happily congratulating himself and clearly enjoyed this process more than any building potential of the blocks.

It was a late winter day warmed by bright sunshine, so we then took a walk together outdoors. I had forgotten that his feet were so much shorter than mine and when he got tired, he simply sat down in the street, looking around for something to do. He was eager to be picked up; I carried him home. During that afternoon I felt our tie to each other had strengthened, and I enjoyed telling his parents about my time with their happy, curious child. Grandma will always remember that afternoon. I doubt he will.

The idea that all we have is now, right now, not the past nor the future, has been said in different ways by many authors. It's true, but it doesn't just apply to actual events. Memories can be stored, and taken out at will, even if no one else who was there remembers. And they can be brought out and enjoyed over and over again. For that, too, I am grateful.

CHILDISH TOYS FOR GROWN-UPS

"When I became a man, I put away childish things, including the fear of childishness," C.S. Lewis once wrote. I agree that we don't need to fear childish things. Perhaps we can benefit from seeking them out and adapting them.

I recently watched my youngest grandchild, 10 months old, gleefully playing in a Jolly Jumper, a seat that looks like a child's swing. It's hung from the ceiling, with the child placed inside so that their feet touch the ground. When he (or she) pushes down, the seat briefly springs upward before gravity brings it down. I remember how much his mother loved it when she was his age. It gives a child a sense of control over their body, and a feeling of pleasure from the repeated bounces. I think that adults, even older adults like me, would like something like the Jolly Jumper. A Jolly Jumper for grownups! It is good exercise, you can control the level of force that you exert, there is no risk of falling, and if you get tired, you can just take a nap where you are.

There may be other childish things that are good for grown-ups, even though some may require modifications. I have a catch-type game that I used to play with another grandchild that consists of two round disks, about six inches in diameter, with a band on the back that the hand fits in. The front of the disk is covered with Velcro, and the game comes with a ball with a fuzzy covering. To play, you need to stand several feet apart; one person throws the ball and the other simply sticks out the disk to catch the ball in the Velcro. You then pull the ball off the Velcro to toss it back. The only problem with extended play is that if you often miss catching the ball you may have to walk a distance to get it and then bend down to pick it up. This disadvantage could be remedied by having a larger Velcro-covered catcher's disk mitt, perhaps as much as three feet in diameter. This would greatly increase your chances of catching the ball, thus reducing the need to run and bend to pick it up. It could also serve as a shield, protecting you from getting hit by the ball!

I have always found that there were two main pleasures in playing this game: the satisfaction of hearing the thud sound when the ball hits the disk, and having conversations with my grandchild while playing. The revised game could increase both of these pleasures.

Another suggestion for adapting a game from childhood for adults was made by my friend Tanya. One of her favorite toys in childhood was the Slinky. This is a helical spring toy, that "walks" down a flight of stairs, going end-over-end as gravity brings it down. This is always great fun to watch. A disadvantage as we get older is that while you can still enjoy seeing the Slinky go down a staircase, to keep playing you would need to go down the stairs to retrieve it, and then walk up the stairs to start the process again. Tanya's suggestion is to tie a long string to the Slinky so that once it finished going down the staircase, a gentle pull will bring it back to your starting position at the top of the stairs. Of course, you would need to attach the string so that it would not get caught in the Slinky as it moved, but I think this is possible.

Some of the adaptations of toys for adults may lose the benefit of providing exercise. But if you find this is so, you can get into your Jolly Jumper to safely move around a bit. And once you get tired out, remember that you can take a nap in it.

One of my own favorites from childhood is the Busy Box. These are colorful plastic toys, usually rectangular, with an assortment of doors to open, figures to squeak, or buttons to push that cause objects to pop out. Years ago, I kept one in my office. In times of stress, I used it to give myself a break, take it out, and have a good laugh. It also helped me focus my thoughts, and if a colleague called or wanted to meet I could in complete honesty say, "Sorry, I'm busy."

I had a Busy Box for many years, but lost track of it after several office moves. But now, in retirement, while I have much to engage me, a Busy Box may be just the thing when I don't feel like doing chores around the house. "Sorry dear, I'm just too busy."

Of course, with current technology, some of the items in Busy Boxes could be made more interesting to adults. They could include a changing array of challenging puzzles to solve, games to play, and information to learn. We might even use it to communicate with others. Come to think of it, maybe we all already have adult Busy Boxes in our iPhones and haven't left this toy behind in childhood after all.

What's the lesson here? Find things that you enjoy, whatever your age, and regardless of the age group they were developed for. You can use them yourself or take them out when you have a friend or a grandchild visiting. And even if some playthings from childhood are no longer very practical, like a Jolly Jumper, you may find, as I did, that just thinking about it and envisioning using it, gives you pleasure.

* * *

My New Housemate

I have a new housemate. My son-in-law, Jay, recently decided to update my Wi-Fi and bought me a Google Nest with a Wi-Fi Router and Point. In case you, like me, had no idea what this was, it consists of two items that are about three inches high and three inches in diameter. They look like big white powder puffs. Jay installed the router in the room where we have our desktop computers, and the point in the living room. These will, he assures me, improve my Wi-Fi service on my desk top computers and improve service for anything that uses the internet, including our iPhones and Netflix. Sounds great to me.

Then Jay mentioned that the item in the living room could answer any questions, using Google on the internet. I just needed to say, "Okay, Google," and she (he gave her a female voice) would give me the answer. And I could also ask her to play any music I wanted to hear, accessed from a streaming service called Pandora.

Huh? Although a friend of mine has Amazon Alexa, which is somewhat similar to the Google

Nest system, I hadn't paid much attention to it when visiting her. This new system in my home at first seemed like a stranger had come to live with us.

In the first two days I asked my Google Nest for the weather several times and asked her to play 50s oldies. I also asked her the capitals of several countries, just to see if she knew them. When she answered it felt magical, as though I had a benevolent wise visitor in my home.

The first two nights I said good night when I left the living room to go to bed, wondering if she would be lonely through the night.

It's now a week later, and I still want to say "thank you" after she answers any question. Most days I try to think up questions I want to ask so she doesn't feel neglected. If I say, "Okay Google "while she is talking, she will stop. I like that feature as I know from experiences with past housemates that it's sometimes hard to get them to stop talking. And there's no hard feelings from my Google Nest.

Also, as it's only my husband and me at home, I can now enjoy having another woman in the house. She's always there, tries to answer anything I ask, and asks nothing of me. What a wonderful gift!

Yesterday I heard my husband talking with her. We were each reading in separate rooms in our apartment. When I heard his voice, it took a few minutes before I realized who he was talking to. I asked what he wanted to know and he said it was a question that was in a crossword puzzle. So, it looks like we have a housemate who can engage with us in some of the activities we like to do. Wow! Even though I have been Googling on my computers and phones for many years, somehow the availability of a voice-activated responsive tool that can answer most of the questions I pose boggles my mind. When I think of the time spent in my younger years looking up answers in dictionaries and encyclopedias, however, not all of it was wasted. I often came across something I was interested in that had nothing to do with what I was looking up, which stirred my curiosity.

I wanted to come up with a name for my Google Nest. I asked her for her preference, but she said she couldn't answer that. Since she is a housemate for my husband and me, we both discussed it, and selected Golda as her name. Golda Meier is one of my heroines, and since my husband and I are both Jewish, it seemed like having a wise woman in our home who is familiar with our cultural backgrounds would be desirable. As I get older and can't remember who starred in a favorite movie, or a figure in history, Golda is likely to be especially helpful. That will truly be a service. Welcome to our home, Golda.

LATE BLOOMER

The expression "late bloomer" is used to describe someone who fulfills their potential later than usual. It can apply to an adolescent who goes through puberty later than expected, or a young adult who finds a career path later than his or her peers. It is rarely used for a senior, yet I believe that for some of us, late blooming can occur after 65. For me, it was only after the responsibilities of a busy life—working hard as a student through graduate school, finding a partner and getting married, getting established in a productive career, and raising children—that I could fully look inward to begin to understand what parts of myself had been neglected. I wanted to find what else life had to offer, and what I wanted to nurture and develop in myself. Although I retired from my career as a research scientist several years ago, I did not feel that my involvement in life was diminishing in interests or activities. In fact, I was just getting started.

I had a dear aunt who lived a full life, with career, spouse and children, and died at 90. She had a loving relationship with her husband, but he always seemed to be the decision maker as to what they would do and who they would visit. He also was the primary spokesperson for both of them, and she often seemed reticent to speak when she was with him. She lovingly cared for him in his final years and had many wonderful memories of their more than 50 years of marriage. After a period of mourning she began seeing her friends and family, and attended cultural events, including jazz concerts, that she so loved throughout her life. During this time, she told me that she felt like a rose that was just starting to open up. How wonderful I thought: at last she felt free and open to the world, and ready to experience it even more fully than in her earlier years.

Perhaps it is when we are finished with many of the tasks and responsibilities that life gives us—

some chosen and some not—that we can appreciate what life has to offer. It is time to find and enjoy those parts of us that have been unexplored.

So I now choose to apply a "late bloomer" status to myself and other seniors who initiate or explore interests and activities that we didn't have the time to do when we were younger.

Abi Gezundt was one of the Yiddish expressions my mother would say about things she was planning, meaning *as long as she stayed healthy.* Health and energy are certainly concerns as I get older. But activities that in the past I could complete in a morning, like visiting several exhibits in a museum, I can now do over two or three days. Also, there are more options available for some activities, including attending virtual classes in new areas of interest, rather than having to go in person.

Certainly, at some point in life, some ambitions and desires may pass the blooming possibilities, especially those that require physical stamina—like becoming a marathon runner—or that involve many years of training and education that no longer seem possible, like becoming a physician. That said, Alan Petricoff ran the NYC marathon in 2022 at age 88, and Atomic Leow was 66 in 2015 when he graduated from medical school in Romania.

I am ready to explore, and have started some new activities, including volunteer work with immigrants, writing a blog, and visiting people and cultural sites that I never had time to explore in the past. And I and a friend have taken on the goal of walking across all the bridges that lead out of Manhattan, which I see as a symbol of my plans for new journeys, some not yet identified. I always liked the Charles Aznavour song "Yesterday, When I Was Young," and felt especially wistful at the line: "There are so many songs in me that won't be sung". But perhaps that doesn't have to be true after all. We can all sing longer and later than we ever anticipated.

Embracing the Aging Role

I have had many roles in life— daughter, mother, wife, scientist, neighbor, friend, and others. In every case, I had some choices about how to play the role, even though there were some requirements or expectations. Now that I have moved into an aging role, I'm not sure how I want to play that part. So as a social scientist, I looked for some guidance. The sociologist Talcott Parsons wrote about the "sick role," which has particular rights and obligations based on social norms. As being sick is not within one's control, we have the "right" to be exempt from normal social roles and a "right" to be taken care of by others, but we also have an "obligation" to make an effort to get better, including seeking help and following medical advice.

At first I didn't see how Parsons' work about the sick role could apply to the aging role. Unlike the temporary nature of many sicknesses, there is no possibility of recovering from aging. However, as I get older, I realize that there are certain rights I can claim as I age. First, I have the right to exempt myself from many of my prior social roles, and allow others to take care of them. I used to hold family get-togethers — birthdays, Passover Seders, Thanksgiving, Hannukah — in my home, taking responsibility for all preparations including most of the cooking. Now that my children are older, they have taken over most of these holiday celebrations, and I usually make or buy a contribution for the meal. I like this change: I have no stress involving meal preparation, and it gives me more time to spend with family at the event.

There are other activities that I exempt myself from by paying others to do them for me, like housecleaning and laundry. In addition, living in a well-serviced apartment building, there are porters and other staff who repair appliances or change ceiling lights so that we don't have to climb up a ladder.

Until recently, I thought that I should always be able to do all these household activities. But I no longer feel that not doing them means I am lazy or shirking responsibilities, or that it is a sign of weakness. Letting others do them is my "right" as part of the aging role. And a bonus is that there are people eager to do these activities for me.

There are also some obligations in the aging role. But rather than requirements, I see them as voluntary and recommended activities. Since there are people who may need to help take care of me if I have medical needs, I am obliged to take care of my health. This past year I had an annual check-up, had cataract surgery, got hearing aids, and was treated for Paget's disease, to prevent bone fractures. Taking care of these health needs is helpful to me and improved my quality of life. My self-care also lessens possible burdens for people who care about me.

But wait, something's missing. Parsons described the sick role as a form of societal deviance, and focused on norms regarding its limitations and requirements. But the aging role is not deviant, and it can provide an opportunity for many life choices, especially after retirement. In a previous essay I wrote about "Managing Successful Aging" and the importance of engagement in life, and I am discovering what that means to me. Playing the aging role is much more than a set of rights and obligations, and I have found that I have many choices of how to play that role.

I have started new activities, like writing and exploring New York City. I have reached out to support friends and family, including spending more time with my husband. Our appreciation for each other and the life we have together after 40+ years of marriage has grown. And I have become more active in my community, getting to know others who are also playing the aging role. We share information, laughter, and ideas, and provide support when a loved one becomes ill or dies.

I will embrace the aging role. The role has rights and obligations, some of which are beneficial to me, and I will follow those social norms. Most importantly, the role has given me an opportunity to make choices and create my own complex, multi-layered life with purpose. After all, in this role not only am I playing the lead, but my part has a limited run, and there are no revivals.

COMFORTS OF LIFE

As I get older, I am more aware of my "comfort objects." These are items that I am familiar with and that I know I like. They help me feel relaxed and calm, as if my needs, and any hurts, are being taken care of. I find that just their presence is comforting, providing solace if anything upsetting is happening in my life.

Certain foods provide examples of these. Like having Rice Krispies cereal with raisins for breakfast or a hot dog on a bun, with mustard and sauerkraut, for lunch. How plebeian, non-gourmet and somewhat unhealthy these are! They make me feel a little guilty because I know, and generally eat, better choices. But there is something about these foods that are tied to pleasure for me from childhood. Perhaps because when my harsh, non-demonstrative mother went food shopping, she occasionally brought me home a hot dog for lunch. I liked the taste and I saw it as a much sought-after expression of her love. It also helped me feel closer to her, and more forgiving. And it still brings me comfort.

For my husband, Doug, a grilled cheese sandwich served with a cup of tomato soup fills the same niche. When he is tired, or after a challenging morning, this lunch comforts and soothes him. He remembers this as a favorite when he was growing up, and perhaps he too associates it with maternal love as well as nourishment.

But it's not just foods that are comfort objects. Doug and I also have our comfort TV shows. We like reruns of *Law and Order*, especially the earlier episodes; the familiarity of the plots, the characters, and the music, can all give comfort. And when Lennie Briscoe (Jerry Orbach) makes a sarcastic remark about a suspected criminal or Jack McCoy

(Sam Waterston) makes a self-righteous speech about ethical issues, it makes me feel like there is goodness and justice in the world. Marathons of this show mean that we can watch several episodes in a row, lulling us into a state of stupor; the day's unpleasantries can be briefly forgotten. Doug also likes *NCIS* reruns, and I can find comfort in a New York Mets baseball game. Fortunately we have two televisions so, when needed, we can engage in our own pleasures.

Clothes too are comfort objects for me. As a professional I often wore suits to work, always with nylon stockings and heels, all clothes that I found somewhat constricting. Since retiring I never wear suits; stockings and heels only come out for special events like weddings. I still dress what may be called "business casual," or "smart casual" when I am out of the house, but when I am home, a comfortable polo shirt, sweatpants, and a hoodie when it's cool, are my favorites. I love the feel of the soft clothes on my body, with no restraints on my movements. Although these items are called activewear, and sometimes I wear them to the gym, I mostly wear them when I am not at all active, and just spending the day at home.

I often enjoy challenges and new experiences, but sometimes familiar comforts are what I need.

* * *

HALF-BIRTHDAYS AND OTHER OPPORTUNITIES FOR CELEBRATION

As I get older, I want to find opportunities for celebration——dare I say it—of me. Like most others, my life has been filled with moments of joy and feelings of accomplishment, and times of grief and feelings of self-doubt. I have decided to find ways to increase the times for celebrations. I'm sure the negative experiences will take care of themselves.

As a wife and parent in my personal life, and a research director and supervisor in my work life, I participated in and often initiated celebrations of others. I enjoyed them all. Generally, they were for life's milestones, like ages reached and weddings, or for work-related accomplishments, such as promotions. Now that I am out of the formal work environment, and have passed many of my own landmarks, there are fewer opportunities for celebrations. I want to find ways I can celebrate myself. I recently celebrated my half-birthday. Interestingly, when you ask a parent the age of their infant or toddler child, they are likely to report it in weeks if the child is under three months of age, or in months if he/she is under two years old. This may be because of the many important developmental milestones that occur during these short time periods. After the second birthday, ages are usually marked and discussed in terms of whole years. But I think we should look at further delineations of age at the other end of life too. For example, I think birthdays should be celebrated biannually after age 75. After all, one is increasingly aware that the numbers left to celebrate are diminishing, so why not celebrate them in smaller increments? I'm not talking about big get-togethers or elaborate affairs, unless that is your choice; it's not mine. I mean simply taking note of the new milestone, congratulating yourself on reaching it, and doing something to celebrate: a glass of wine, a special meal, buying something you have wanted, or arranging a date with a beloved friend. Of course one can celebrate birthdays in even greater frequency. But I personally would not go as far as Lewis Carroll suggested in *Through the Looking Glass*, celebrating an "unbirthday" 364 days a year. I think too much celebrating would diminish the celebratory feelings.

In my recent half-birthday celebration, I had my Google Nest sing Happy Birthday to me in the morning and met a friend for lunch. At dinner with my husband we had some Prosecco and I blew out a candle on my blueberry pie and ice-cream dessert. A satisfying celebration indeed.

I also found other days that I can celebrate myself, days dedicated to various roles that fit me, related to my senior status. They include Grandma's Day (January 21), National Senior Citizen's Day (August 21), and National Grandparents Day (September, the first Sunday after Labor Day). The UN has even declared October 1st an International Day of Older Persons. So if I feel like it, I may choose to celebrate myself on one of those days in the future. May is also an Older Americans Month, but since May has Mother's Day, perhaps that one day for celebrating me in May is sufficient. However, I can pick another one or two other days in

May, and perhaps invite another Older American to celebrate with me!

There are also activities I do that have official dates of recognition. For example. I enjoy writing non-fiction, and found there is a National Authors' Day (Nov 1). I also volunteer with an organization serving immigrants, and recently learned about Volunteer Recognition Day (April 20).

I look forward to many opportunities for celebrations throughout the year.

THANKFUL THAT NOTHING HAPPENED

I am learning that sometimes I should be grateful that nothing happened. Let me explain. One recent week had many sources of distress. I thought I lost my building entry card that has my photo on it and would involve cost and time to get replaced. I was annoyed. Also, I couldn't access my Masterclass on-line classes. I called the customer service line but they couldn't help me, even after giving me a new password. Not only were they not helpful—but after following all their instructions, I believed I lost other automatic passwords on my computer thus leaving me worse off than when I started. I was upset. That same day, after returning from getting a haircut, my husband announced that he had lost his wallet—filled with credit cards and ID cards— a nightmare to replace, and potentially costly. And one more thing: earlier in the week I went for a physical exam, as I had been feeling very tired in the past few months, and I needed to call my doctor for the results of my blood tests. I had some concern that some disease or deficit would be found in these tests, changing my life.

So what happened? After looking in the various compartments of my pocketbook multiple times, I found the ID card— I must have missed one compartment. The morning after the Masterclass problem I turned on my computer with trepidation, prepared to call the customer service line again, and voilà—I could access Masterclass, and everything else seemed to be functioning okay. Then I searched my husband's coats and pants pockets for the wallet, to no avail, but walking through the living room I saw the wallet tucked into the side of a chair. In searching his pockets, it must have fallen out and gotten wedged next to the pillow. And at the end of the week I called my doctor and learned that all my tests were normal.

All this helped me realize that feeling good should not just come from appreciating the good things in life that can happen, like having a nice dinner with a close friend or hearing that one of my children got a promotion. I should also feel pleasure when something that could have potentially gone bad, didn't go bad, or when there has been an absence of bad news: potential disasters averted. During that entire week, any one of those things I worried about could have turned out poorly— but nothing happened. Even more important, there was no bad news, like calls that someone was ill.

So, I can still hope for good things happening, like visits from people I have been eager to see, and wedding plans or promotions among family and friends. But some days I plan to just sit back and appreciate that while there is often potential for various things to go wrong, nothing bad has happened.

FAMILY MATTERS

ACROSS THE AGES

My newest grandson, Lucas, is five months old, and has become responsive to my talking and smiling. He spends much of his waking time, when he is not being fed or diapered, kicking his feet in the air, waving his arms, and making cooing sounds. What a pleasure to watch. I eagerly anticipate spending time with him as he grows up.

As Lucas is at the very beginning of his life, and I have gone through the majority of my life stages, I thought about our differences and similarities and wondered whether we can connect across our ages. I think we can. The differences are many, but I expect some will diminish.

Lucas has no words yet, and I am a logophile. I love reading, writing, and especially finding the right words to express my thoughts. I will teach him new words, and how to play Scrabble, my favorite game, as we both age. And as he becomes familiar with new technologies or new terms entering our culture, he can teach me those.

He can't walk. Actually, he can't even crawl yet. I love to go for long walks, and to visit new museums and other places. As we both age our mobility capacities or incapacities will coincide. His little legs will mean he can't cover too much distance too quickly, and this will match the distance I can cover with my flagging energy. I hope we will go to many places together.

He sleeps a lot now but will soon require less sleeping time, and will nap infrequently. And though I am busy and active throughout the day, I am approaching the time when occasional daytime naps will help me feel refreshed, so maybe we'll nap at the same time.

And there are similarities which are likely to become differences:

He eats often, about every three to four hours. As he gets older, he will need to eat less frequently.

Since I retired, and was home more during Covid lockdown, I too eat about every three to four hours, whereas I used to just eat at mealtimes, about every six to seven hours. Will my new eating pattern continue? I'm not sure. If so, we have another similarity: we both seem to be outgrowing our clothes! Our bland diets are somewhat similar now. Lucas is just on milk, and I prefer mild, non-spicy, delicate flavors. This will definitely change for Lucas as his parents love many cuisines, some of which are quite spicy, and they will introduce him to all of them. And I will introduce him to some of our family's favorite foods, like bagels and noodle pudding, in moderation of course.

Lucas' hair has been thinning since his birth, and it will soon begin filling in, as his parents both have thick hair. My hair is thinning as well, but I expect the change for me is unidirectional.

We both stay home much of the time now. Before Covid I traveled extensively, both for work and pleasure, but Covid and retirement means that home and family-based activities have increased. This is likely to continue. Lucas' Mom's profession is in International Development, and his parents look forward to showing him the world. He has much travel in his future. I look forward to hearing about his travels when he gets home.

Bubba's Legacy

Her smell always comforted me. It reminded me of warm, soft, freshly cleaned blankets. When I was seven and eight years old I would get into bed with her if I had had a difficult day or felt sad. She never asked me why, but she always had open arms. Only five feet tall, with long gray hair, she was my comforter and protector through most of my childhood.

She wore her hair combed back and wound into a bun, held secure with long gray hairpins. Sometimes she let me make two braids that I pinned to the top of her head. She never seemed to mind when I fixed her hair that way, but always took out the braids and returned her hair to its usual style before leaving her bedroom.

Bubba, the word for grandmother in Yiddish, was my maternal grandmother, and lived with my family from the time she came to the United States from Poland in the 1920s, when she was in her early 50s, until she entered a nursing home in her final year of life, about thirty years later. She was born in Krasneshiltz, Poland, a two-day buggy ride from Warsaw. As a child, hearing her stories, I often wondered if almost every place in Poland was a two-day buggy-ride from Warsaw. Bubba had nine children and was widowed at thirty nine when her husband died suddenly. She came to New York to live with my mother and our family after all her children had left home. My mother asked her to come to take care of her newborn, my older sister.

I was the youngest of three children and we lived above my father's dry goods store in Williamsburg Brooklyn. Bubba never learned to speak English, so Yiddish was the language at home, but she did have an American sounding given name: Dora (Devorah in Hebrew).

She helped my mother with childcare and housekeeping activities, as my parents often worked in the store together. I remember her cabbage soup and stuffed cabbage, but I never recorded those recipes. I do still make her noodle pudding, and before I entered the recipe into my computer, I kept it in my calendar book under "assets."

Bubba enjoyed watching television in the evening and believed that because she could see the people on TV, they saw us too. She became very upset if I started to undress to change into my pajamas while watching evening TV. *"VUS TIST DEE?"* she would ask. What are you doing? *"GAY AROIS."* Go out. She didn't want the man on the TV to see me.

My mother bought a black upright piano when I was about four or five. Piano lessons were first given to my older sister and brother, and when they both refused to continue these lessons, it was up to me. I didn't feel I had a choice, and in addition to the weekly lessons, I was expected to practice one hour daily. I never enjoyed practicing; I wanted to do my homework or play. If my mother thought I had not practiced for a full hour she would yell at me: "Practice." Bubba would say, *"LUHZ ER TSRI."* Leave her alone. Then she told my mother that I had finished one full hour of practice before she came home. This appeased my mother. I loved Bubba for her protection and the secret we shared.

For most of the time she lived with us, until walking became too difficult, Bubba went to the Orthodox Synagogue every Saturday. When she could no longer go, she would sit in her rocking chair reading her prayer books, at peace in the world. She was always peaceful.

In the last two years of her life, she had dementia. Although she had been our primary cook, she now began burning food on the stove. I was surprised when I saw her open the refrigerator to drink from a ketchup bottle. As her condition deteriorated, she would go out on the street and forget her way home. The police department would call and my mother would go to the station to bring her home.

No longer at peace, often distressed, some evenings she would put her head out of our apartment window calling for my brother, concerned that he was out with a *"SHIKSA,"* a non-Jewish girl.

Bubba's behavior became very difficult for my mother to manage at home, especially after my father died. About a year after his death, my mother moved Bubba to a nursing home. Although I visited Bubba in the nursing home, I only have a vague recollection of those visits. I remember that it was crowded and smelled of urine and cleaning solution. She died within a year of that move. I was fourteen.

I never told her how much she meant to me. I like to think that she knew. When my daughter was born, almost 40 years ago, and more than 20 years after Bubba died, I named her Dara and gave her Bubba's Hebrew name, Devorah. Dara is as loving and protective as her great-grandmother was. Their similarities are striking and I see them in every part of Dara's life, especially in her relations with her family, friends, and her colleagues in international development work. I realize that growing up around the turn of the 21st century, Dara has had many advantages Dora could never have had. Still, the thread of connection is there, and although they never met, Dara has inherited the legacy of Bubba's love, through me. I take pleasure in knowing that I have transmitted some benefits from my childhood to my children, and perhaps through them, even to future generations. And it's not too late to say it. "Thank you, Bubba. I love you."

ME COMPETITIVE?

I never felt competitive when I was in school. I studied hard and worried about my grades, and I usually did very well on tests. I didn't feel competitive in sports either. I remember playing ping pong and tennis with my family, but I was a middling player, so I never aspired to be a consistent winner.

When I played with my children, it was more as a means to have conversations than to win. And my husband was so much better than me in these sports that when I played with him I just did it for the exercise. I wasn't competitive at work either. While being a research scientist meant that part of my job was to submit grant proposals, as did many scientists hoping to get funding, I never felt I was in direct competition with others. I believed that there was sufficient money for all the best proposals to get funded.

As I get older, I am beginning to recognize that maybe I *am* competitive. I like word games, including Words with Friends, Scrabble and Boggle. When I win, I feel magnanimous, attributing it to luck or long experience. But when I lose, I feel a little depressed for a while. Even when I play with people close to me, like my children, I am happy for their win, but am eager to play again to at least "even it up." I suppose I was always competitive in word games; I just couldn't admit it before. Actually, as I think about this, maybe I was competitive in other aspects of my life too—work achievements, looks, home furnishings—I just can't admit that either.

A new arena for competition emerged a few years ago when I met my new *machetayneste,* the Yiddish word for the mother of one's child's spouse. There is no English equivalent, perhaps attesting to the greater importance of this connection in the Jewish tradition. There's even a Yiddish song: *Machetayneste Mayne* (*mayne* implying my dear). It's about a mother who wants her daughter's mother-in-law to treat her daughter well.

After my daughter and her boyfriend got engaged, a dinner was arranged for the in-laws to meet—my husband and I, our daughter, her soon-to-be-husband, and his parents. The dinner was very cordial, everyone happy to be together, and the parents were happy that their children were very much in love. But I noticed that the *machetayneste* was younger and thinner than me, and had an attractive, well-coiffed hairstyle, while my curly hair is not easy to manage. She also had a lovely Southern accent, having lived in Virginia her entire life. I knew that my Brooklyn accent, less sweet-sounding, was still with me even though I had moved away from Brooklyn decades ago. Meeting her and anticipating ongoing contact was a new experience for me, as my other child's mother-in-law was living in Columbia, so the distance and our language differences meant that contact would be limited.

The next meeting was when my *machetayneste* (Nora) and I went with our children to explore wedding venues. We all stayed together in an Airbnb and Nora brought lots of snacks, including wine for us to share. I had not thought of bringing food and anticipated that we would buy what we wanted for the house together, and eat most meals out. Was I competing in hospitality? And when we went into one of the wedding venues, Nora gracefully insisted that I go first, referring to me as the "important mother." Wow! Was I less gracious too?

I decided to try to relax and enjoy this special trip. But as we drove around to visit places and talked about the wedding, Nora mentioned her desire to lose weight before the event. I hadn't given much thought to this, as the event was about a year off. But since she was already thinner than me, I said I planned to lose weight too. I then playfully said that I would send her cookies for the upcoming holiday season. We both laughed. But when the holiday came, we sent cookies and cakes to each other. Perhaps she felt a little competitive too.

The wedding was lovely. I think we both had lost a few pounds, probably not enough for anyone to notice. About 13 months later our grandson was born. Nora asked to be called *Nana* and I said *Grandma* was fine for me; we were glad we would have different names. We love our grandson very much, and we each try and see him every few weeks. Based on the pictures my daughter posts, I know that both Nora and I regularly send or bring our shared grandson clothes and toys. Perhaps I even feel a little competitive about what I bring him, since last time I visited I made a kugel, a noodle pudding, using my Polish grandmother's recipe. My daughter loves it and I hope my grandson will too. And I know that Nora makes and brings delicious Southern delicacies when she visits them.

I have concluded that my *machetayneste* and I have similar, and unique, ways of showing our grandson and his family the love we feel for them. There may be a little competition involved some-times, but that will be fine, as it also represents a lifetime collaboration that we all welcome.

Mixed Food Groups

Having a family dinner party years ago used to be a rather simple activity. I have a large extended family, so the first step was deciding who to invite. After that I could pretty much make whatever I wanted to serve and the main question was how much food to prepare. But as my children have grown, and their partners have been added to our dinners, things have gotten complicated; food choices have become more selective. Recently, a few of us were going to a Mets baseball game, and seven family and friends were in my home for drinks and hors d'oeuvres prior to leaving for the game together. It seemed simple. My husband and I are omnivores, as were two of the guests. But of the other three, one was a pescatarian (I bought shrimp), one a vegetarian (vegetables and crackers needed for the dips), and the last one doesn't eat fish (cheese and prosciutto was fine). And almost everyone was trying to lose weight (double up on the dip vegetables). This need to consider the mixture of dietary choices is not new to me. My larger family group includes a vegan, a vegetarian who doesn't eat cheese, and several who have been on a gluten-free diet.

Growing up in a kosher Jewish household, there was never a choice of what to eat; you ate what was served. The separation of dairy and meat dishes, part of the *kashruth mandate,* further limited our meals. I knew not to ask for sour cream for a potato if I was eating chicken for dinner. Also, some kind of animal-based protein was always a required part of any meal—chicken, beef or fish.

My parents were immigrants from Europe, lived through the Depression, and made it into the middle class through hard work, when there was little awareness of cholesterol or fatty foods as a health concern. Meat was the most coveted main dish, and feeling full after a meal was desirable and meant that the meal was successful.

So, what's a mother to do with mixed food groups in the family? There are several options that I have used: vegetable pasta dishes (with a non-dairy cheese to substitute for the parmigiana cheese) works for everyone, except those who want animal protein; making different dishes for different folks (the most demanding of time); or ordering food from a restaurant, for everyone, or just special dishes for those who don't eat fish or meat (a costlier option). The costliest, but one that seems to work well, is having dinner at a restaurant that has a broad assortment of dishes; Italian, Middle Eastern or Thai food tend to be best for this. The disadvantage to eating in a restaurant is that the time we can all spend together may be limited, especially if it is a busy place seeking to serve as many patrons as possible. Also, the guests are likely to stay in their initial seats, perhaps making it difficult to talk with others at the table. I guess there's no perfect solution.

During Covid, my family had virtual dinners. The main role of the host at those events was to send out the invitations. Once folks were gathered, each providing their own foods, they also had responsibility for serving themselves and cleaning up. Although there are some definite advantages to that, I think we were all eager for in person get-togethers again, even though the menu is always more complicated. And though I continue to ask guests their food choices, just being together is the underlying goal. That's the main item on the menu. Bon Appetit!

The Seder Table

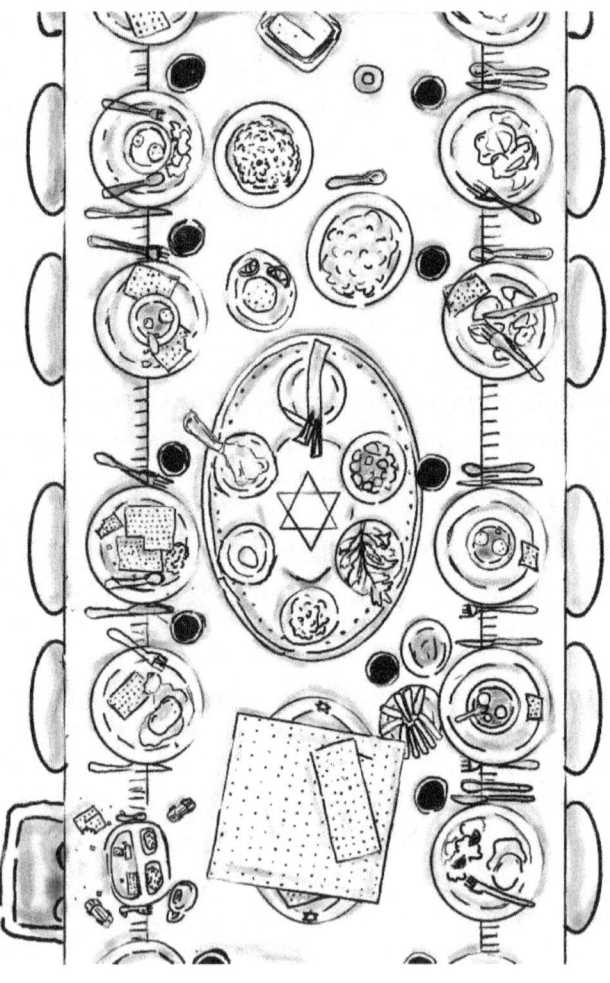

Art by : Juliana Suárez-Lipton

PASSED OVER?

I have participated in an annual Passover Seder all of my life. I grew up in an Orthodox Jewish home, and my mother prepared this ceremonial meal most of her married life, until she ceded the activity to my older sister. After I married, even though my Jewish religious affiliation changed to Reform and then to Humanism, I continued this annual ritual. I looked forward to it as a special time for the entire family to come together. As an adult, I especially enjoyed reading the story of Passover in English; as a child it was in Hebrew, little understood by any of those participating, including me.

I prepared the Seder meal when we had a home in the suburbs and continued after we moved back to New York City. In March 2020, I started planning what I anticipated would be the last Seder I would take responsibility for. Although it was fun to have the family, and sometimes friends, join together and read through the story of Passover, I decided that preparing a multi-course dinner for up to 20 people was something I was ready to give up. I asked my newly married daughter, Dara, who loves the Seder ritual, to take it over starting the following year, and I began planning for the upcoming event.

The Seder was to be in early April, on the first night of the Passover holiday. But in late March, after talking with the family, we decided to cancel the in-person event. The fear of Covid transmission and warnings against large gatherings led to the cancellation, especially since some family members are seniors and some are immunocompromised.

Dara took over organizing a virtual Seder. She created a modified Haggadah, and we all prepared by having wine and matzoh ready. As is our family's custom, we each read part of the Passover story. At the end, as we said good-bye, we discussed having an in-person Seder at my daughter's home in 2021. She was pregnant at the time, and we all anticipated having a new youngest family member to play with.

Much happened during that year, both in the pandemic and in our family. Covid cases declined and the vaccine became widely available. But not everyone in the family got vaccinated and large gatherings were still discouraged. And so, we planned our second virtual Seder.

My daughter hosted the virtual ceremony, with her new son, our youngest attendee.

Four members of our family contracted Covid that year. In the Haggadah, Passover refers to the Jews who were passed over from the consequences of one of the plagues. I am grateful that our family was "passed over" in terms of serious post-Covid effects, and all are now almost fully restored to health. I am sad for those who were not so fortunate.

I am also reminded of another meaning of "passed over": my daughter inherited the responsibility for the Passover Seder tradition, albeit in a virtual state at first. Other family holiday get-togethers are also being passed over. I used to host Thanksgiving and Hannukah too, and was always pleased that the family was brought together and had a good time. Thanksgiving was the first to go: my stepdaughter is an accomplished chef, loves this holiday, and we began going to her home for Thanksgiving several years ago. Hannukah was next. With our children inter-marrying, the holiday became Chrismukkah, and when my daughter-in-law wanted to invite family to see her new home around the holidays, she asked if I minded if she did this annual holiday party in the future also. Fine with me I thought, I can relax and just enjoy the family gathering and I get to bring the potato latkes. The Passover Seder was the last to go and I was ready to cede that holiday too.

This is a reminder that change is part of life and it is good when there are young people eager to continue family traditions. Amen.

JOY FROM NOTHING AND EVERYTHING

I learned something about feeling joy in the moment from my now three year old grandson Lucas recently when he came to visit me with his parents. He is a happy, active child, and enjoys experiencing whatever he finds in life on any particular day. Nothing special happened, yet it was all special.

I took Lucas to the supermarket to get some milk, and decided to walk through every aisle with him. He half-walked, half-ran, eager to pick out all the things he recognized, calling them out with great pleasure: oranges, spaghetti, milk. He especially liked it when I asked him to find something I saw in the aisle before we got to it, like eggs, chips, and ice cream. "I found it!" he called out. What joy he took in the freedom to move through the aisles, to recognize so many items, and find others, in the treasure hunt I had created.

On another day at home with him I decided to do some of my floor exercises, since I knew I would not have time for the gym that day. I invited Lucas to join me. He laid down on the floor next to me. Lying on our backs and lifting our legs into the air was easy for him; his body so much more flexible than mine, and he wiggled his legs as they went up. Getting on our hands and knees I told him to alternate lifting his legs out to the side and I demonstrated what I meant—this exercise is called the fire hydrant— but he alternated kicking his legs up toward the back, gleefully saying, "I did it higher, Grandma.". His pleasure seemed to come from just experiencing his body and attempting to follow my directions. I never laughed so much doing exercises.

He doesn't know that food shopping and exercising are chores, and that I am eager to check them off my list when I get them done. For him, they are just ways he can be himself, enjoying the movements and the stimulation he experiences.

Watching Lucas' glee in the quotidian— experiencing joy that was absolute as he ran down the super-market aisles, and as he moved his body in doing exercises— also brought me joy. And I wondered if I could capture that feeling now in the activities of my life. Perhaps I had it as a child, but as an adult I often feel weighed down with obligations, and with concerns about people who I care about, and about the challenges of aging. These creep into my life, like mud moving on a downslope, covering and coloring everything in its way.

What's the meaning of this for me? I don't expect to start taking pleasure in going down the supermarket aisles or doing my exercises, any more than I have in the past, except perhaps if I think of Lucas and how he enjoyed doing these. This is a joy of grandparenting. But I want to hold on to a belief that even in everyday activities—if I can see them in new ways, and experience my own engagement in them—there is pleasure to be had. Even now.

WHAT WE SAVE, WHAT WE CAST OFF

COLLECTIONS

I have some new interests and need to make room in my apartment for new collections. I like reading biographies and learning more about my city, so I need to make space for books, pamphlets, and other things these interests require. What to discard? Why is this so difficult? I identified two categories of my collections: the "somewhat useless" that can be trimmed back, and the "can't live without them" that are things to keep.

Somewhat Useless Most of the Time

Spare Buttons and Threads

These are the extras that often come with new clothes, like blouses or pants. I have hundreds of these in a big cookie container, most in little plastic bags, but have never used them. Actually, once I did: my six-year-old granddaughter seemed at a loss for what to do when visiting me one day, and I gave her this container. She enjoyed sorting and organizing the buttons, just like I did with my grandmother's collection when I was six or seven. I guess I can't get rid of them.

Chinese Food Condiments and Plastic Implements

I get these when I order Chinese food for delivery to my home, which appears to have been hundreds of times. My favorite Chinese restaurant provides sealed plastic bags with packets of duck sauce, soy sauce and Chinese mustard, along with a small spoon and fork and a tiny, folded paper napkin. I have a large growing collection of these packets on two shelves. Since I eat this food at home, I use my own implements and napkins, especially since the napkins provided are too small for use by anything larger than a small rodent. But it seems a shame to throw any of this out. And one time a few years ago while making a dish that required soy sauce, I used at least 25 of my saved soy sauce packets. And I may want to go on a picnic where the plastic ware will be useful. So, I guess I can't get rid of these things either.

Earrings and Socks

I have quite a few single earrings, but I remain hopeful that one day the lost ones will appear. Many years ago, wearing single earrings was in fashion. Also, why do I feel my earrings have to match? In another drawer, I have a similar collection of single socks, not likely ever to be in style as singletons, but maybe one day the other sock will appear, or I will decide to make some hand puppets. So, I better hold on to those socks too.

Keys

I have several keys, even groups of keys, with no notion of the location of their locks. Some may be from my former house in New Jersey (I moved 12 years ago), or a friend's apartment, an old storage locker, or some other place. Some may have even been left in prior homes I lived in and I kept them just in case I ever needed them, and brought them with me each time I moved. Who knows, one day I may encounter a lock that one of those keys will fit

Greeting Cards

My husband and I contribute to many charities, and many of them provide free greeting cards. Why? I suppose they expect that upon receipt of their cards, additional donations will be sent. Also, since the name of the charity is on the back of the card, they hope that when you send the card you may recruit new donors. These cards include "Happy Birthday," "Get Well," and "Thinking of You" and a particularly large blitz of "Happy Holidays" cards received around Christmas time. My favorites are the all-purpose blank cards with nice pictures of flowers. The growth in our card collection far exceeds my need for their use, even if I decided to send a card every day to everyone I know. Especially useless are the "Thinking of You" variety. If I am thinking of someone I will email or call them. However, I can use the envelopes that come with these cards to mail letters or pay bills, and maybe sometimes I will need one of the cards, so the collection grows.

Can't Live Without Them Because They Comfort Me

Toilet Paper

I get nervous when we are down to only one roll in each of our two bathrooms. I like buying the 12-pack, putting half of the rolls in each bathroom, and then getting extra packs for the linen closet. When the bathrooms are stocked and there are extras in the closet, I feel that one of my primary home-making responsibilities has been fulfilled and I am ready for any number of guests.

Address Labels

This is one of my husband's collections, and is related to the greeting card collection, as many charities send sheets of peel-off address labels that you can use on letters or other mail. Despite my extensive snail mail letter writing/bill paying activities, the address label collection has continued to grow. We could probably paper all the rooms in my apartment with the labels and still have enough for anything we will ever want to mail. But it's comforting to know we will never need to write out our home address. Perhaps one day we will move so that we can throw out this collection.

Batteries

We have a large collection of batteries of various sizes and shapes; D, A, 9V, and others. And though we have purchased batteries for our flashlights, remote controls, night lights, and other uses, when a need arises, we look through our big bag of batteries but never seem to find the right size or the right number of batteries. But we can't throw them out, even though I noticed that some have expiration dates over a decade ago. You never know when they might be needed and they probably still work.

After reviewing these collections, one thing is clear: My new collections will need to find their place within the comfort of the old ones, which will be around for a while.

EXPIRATION DATES

Getting older means that you have lots of things in your home that probably should be thrown out.

Some may even have expiration dates. I have developed some rules for when food or other items can be discarded, as follows:

In the kitchen, discard foods when...

- You don't remember having the original meal that created that particular leftover.

- There's something growing on the food that is a different color than the original item.

- The liquid/sauce that is in the bottle has caked so firmly over the screw cap that you can no longer open the bottle without using carpenters' tools or smashing it against the counter.

- You can no longer read the expiration date.

- It doesn't pass the smell test, although thresholds for this may vary.

In the pantry, discard foods when...

- The can is bulging and threatens to explode.

- It's a food that you don't like, never liked, and will never like. You probably bought it because someone said it was good for you or it was on sale.

- The seasonings/spices have been around so long that they have no aroma and add nothing to the taste of foods, although you can keep some to add a little color to food.

In the medicine chest/bathroom cabinet, discard items when...

- There's a medication or lotion that you remember packing and moving from your last home, and haven't used since, and you moved more than ten years ago.

- They have an expiration date that's more than two years old. Note: This applies to kitchen and pantry too. However, you might want to keep any anti-anxiety medications. Even if they've lost some potency, the placebo effect can be helpful.

In the closet, throw out or give away...

- Clothes you haven't worn for many years. You will never be that size again, and the style is not likely to come back.

- Shoes that are too tight. You may love them, but they hurt your feet whenever they are worn for more than 15 minutes. Your feet will never get smaller.

Congratulations, you have probably now discarded most of what was in your closet.

All around the house, discard...

- Tchotchkes that you don't care about. You don't remember how you got them and you never really liked them. If the people who gave you a tchotchke come to visit, they won't remember what they gave you anyway.

- Piles of papers. If the letter is more than three months old, get rid of it. If it was a bill, they probably sent you a newer bill, with a late fee. You should pay that one. If it's from a charity, don't worry, they will keep sending you solicitations.

- Piles of magazines or newsletters. If you have a subscription just start reading the newer ones and discard the old ones. If you keep postponing reading any of them, cancel the subscription.

And speaking of expiration dates:

I wish... maybe... that I knew the expiration dates for people close to me. If I did, I would know who I wanted to visit soon, and who could wait. I also would know who to make peace with, or who could wait a little longer. And who I still needed to pay back or return/or get back something that was loaned, or not.

As to my own expiration date, I don't want to know that, but if I did, I would want to extend the date, or would I?

BOXED IN

My move from a suburban house back into a city apartment meant that I lost living space and many closets. It was also the end of an era, as my children were grown and living in their own homes, and I was eager to get back to Manhattan. Not only would this eliminate my long commute to work, but I missed the city, having lived there before moving to suburbia when my children were young.

Most of the furniture in our four-bedroom house was given away, some was sold, and we moved into a much smaller, two-bedroom apartment in my old neighborhood, in Manhattan's East Side. Many boxes were packed up for the move, and most came into the apartment to be unpacked and put to use. Others were put in a storage room in my new apartment building. They stayed there until 13 years later.

My husband Doug had recently decided to give up his hobby of making and running miniature war games. This meant that the materials that he kept in a studio where he created the war game scenarios were no longer needed, and neither was the studio. We gave up the studio, and sold much of the materiel (troops, weapons, terrain) he had amassed.

But there were some things he wanted to keep, at least for a while. Since we don't have space in our apartment for these things, we decided that this was an opportunity to go through the boxes that were in the storage room and get rid of things we didn't need and hadn't missed in the years they were in storage. We could then put my husband's war game materials into this storage area until he chose to use them again.

We did it. We enlisted the help of our son, Noah, and his family to move all the boxes from the storage room into our apartment, and then put the boxes from the studio in the storage room.

A total of 18 boxes came from storage into my apartment foyer. There were three or four with tax documents from the last 10 years. I threw out or shredded everything that was more than seven years old. From the more recent tax files, I threw out things that would not be likely to be needed for an audit, like electricity bills and receipts. I'm a bit of a hoarder, so I store all bill-related items with each year's tax folders. Going through these items brought back memories of clothes I bought and the special events they represented, growing children's needs, repairs for the house and medical visits. This took many more hours than I had planned as I savored some memories and resurrected regrets associated with others.

After tossing and shredding tax-related papers, two boxes were gone. This looked promising.

Then the challenges emerged.

My husband had three boxes of research articles written by him and his colleagues from his days as a criminologist/research scientist, all more than 20 years old. He saw these as a treasure trove, with many articles published before the internet, and nowhere else to be found. Determined to find a home for them, Doug called a criminal justice university library to see if they would be interested. They were. But it was during Covid and they were not accepting any donations. Three boxes resided in my foyer for about six months before we were able to deliver them to the university. My husband and I were pleased, for he is reassured that part of his legacy will be sustained.

Then we were down to 13 boxes.

There were lots of family photos, including the baby books I created for my son and daughter. But there were also lots of old photos of my children—school photos, holidays, summer camps. I need to sort them and talk to my children about taking them. There are also photos of my parents, siblings, old friends, dogs I have cherished. Where were they all to go? I can't throw them out.

Memorabilia from my children have a special place in my heart. These include years of Mother's Day cards and letters from sleep away camp. I even found an envelope with short curly dirty blond hair from Noah's first haircut. He's now 41. I showed him some of the letters and the beloved blond locks, but there was not much interest. I can't throw that wonderful treasure box away either.

Sightseeing photos fill another box. For many years, pre-iPhone cameras, I took many pictures when I traveled for work or vacation, often in Europe, and almost always ordered duplicate copies. I kept them all, and the negatives. Many are of places I don't remember, but they are lovely statues, churches, fields, bodies of water. I could throw out the duplicate copies, and the negatives, but that still leaves a boxful. It's not going anywhere yet.

And I don't know what to do with the box full of VCR tapes. Some are classic movies, some are tapes of family parties, including Bar and Bat Mitzvah tapes mainly filled with scenes from the parties we had after the religious ceremonies. All these will have to be turned into discs to be viewable. I will do that sometime. For now, they can stay in the same box with the photos.

Then there are three boxes of tchotchkes that decorated my prior homes and offices. They are mainly travel memorabilia like little mother and child statues and framed family pictures. I no longer have the space to display these things. My diplomas are in this box too. These items represent an important part of my personal and professional identities and experiences.

So, of the 18 boxes, with consolidation, I was down to 12. Not much progress for several months. They sat in my foyer for a while, an interesting array. Some are made of tan cardboard, about 1.5 feet square, some are white file boxes about the same size, and all are a little crushed. They sat piled two or three high, leaning against each other and the foyer wall for support. They waited for me to decide their fate. Finally, although the storage room was almost totally filled with what was in my husband's studio, we decided that with some rearranging, the boxes could go back there. We agreed that we would soon go through them again for one final time.

My daughter has lots of storage space in her basement in Virginia, and when I told her about the boxes, she offered to store them there for me. Now there's a thought.

*   *   *

SHEDDING

I always associated shedding with something animals did, like snakes shedding their skin, or dogs shedding hair. I haven't thought about it for humans until recently, when I became aware of my own shedding activities—the involuntary and the voluntary.

Over the course of my adult life I acquired several homes. When our children were young we bought a vacation home in the Poconos, and soon after we moved from our city apartment to a large home in the suburbs. Several years later, we acquired a condo in Florida, inherited from my mother-in-law. In recent years I have been divesting many of these acquisitions.

The vacation house was the first to go. When my children became high-school age and wanted to stay home on weekends to be with their friends, we decided to sell it. We only had it for a few years and since the house had come furnished, we just left everything behind. Also, we didn't miss the space as we had already moved to our suburban home and it provided many outdoor activities.

About 15 years ago, after the children went to college, we sold our suburban house and moved back to Manhattan. This also was not difficult for me. I was eager to get back to Manhattan and never thought of myself as a suburban Mom. But this was my first major divestment and we had lots to dispose of. Most of the furniture was sold, given to others, donated or thrown out. The new owners bought our dining room set, and we left the backyard furniture; no need for that in a Manhattan high rise apartment. But the basement of the house had provided space for materials for my husband's life-long miniature wargame hobby, and we had no space for it in the new apartment. So we rented a studio in Manhattan where Doug could continue to paint figures, create battlefields, and do other activities needed for use at war-gaming conventions.

The stuff that we never used that was stored in our many closets was easy to part with. In the last few days we lived there, since we were required to leave the house "broom-clean," we got a big dumpster and threw things out of the window from the second floor. This was fun. After all these years, I haven't missed anything I gave up, although I could use some of that lost closet space.

The next major real estate divestment occurred when we closed the studio Doug used for his hobby. His energy level had declined and he was ready to give up this hobby. We prepared an inventory of all his materials, troops and weaponry, war by war, mostly naval, WWII and the American Civil War. He shared these lists with fellow-wargamers and was able to sell most of the troops and gaming materials. I often joked with friends that it wasn't easy to provide a home for thousands of troops, nor to see them go off to an unknown future. When I asked Doug if it was difficult to give up the studio and its contents, he looked at me with surprise. I think that since most of the troops were sold to friends, he draws comfort from knowing where his troops are living now and that they are cared for.

The most recent shedding was the selling of our Florida condo apartment. We used it infrequently, mainly to visit relatives who live in Florida. There are upkeep costs for an aging property that don't seem worth it anymore, and it will be less costly for us to stay in hotels or with family when we visit. But this was not as easy as the other divestments; my mother-in-law had collected many fine Asian furniture and decorative pieces, some of which we grew to cherish. My husband and I have selected several pieces we want, and as for the rest, my children created an inventory of items and each selected what they wished to take. The rest was sold, given away or donated.

This process has got me thinking about divestment generally. Giving up the homes I lived in has not been very difficult, perhaps because each change was something I chose. Many of the items I cared about I have kept or I will be able to visit at my children's homes.

When I retired I continued consulting for a while but I no longer engage in many of the activities I once did, including writing research articles, overseeing the activities of a research center, and making presentations at research conferences. Shedding my professional role came with mixed feelings.

As I mentioned in an earlier essay, I used to hold family holiday get-togethers in my home, like Thanksgiving, Hannukah and Passover. All these holiday events have been taken over by my children.

So what is left after these many divestments of homes and their contents, of work and its activities, and of holiday functions in the family? There was a temporary sense of loss and sadness when some of these changes happened; I was wistful when I left the home where my children grew up and felt a sense of loss when I retired from my research position and when I stopped making holiday dinners. But as time goes by, I don't experience these changes as losses. I have more time to explore things that interest me and I know that my experiences and accomplishments will always be part of who I am. And who I am is more than these accomplishments, and continues to change.

But I have found that the process of shedding some long-held ideas and concepts about myself is harder to accomplish. In past years I thought of myself as a superwoman of sorts, and readily undertook multiple activities simultaneously, including caring for my family and managing a busy career. Now I have had to shed the idea of having limitless energy. I am replacing this with a new concept of myself—someone with more time, and with roles and capacities that didn't seem possible before. Perhaps this shedding is really trading many of my former activities for new ones, and I am creating a differently composed superwoman.

I recently read that when snakes grow, their skin does not, so they have to shed their outer layer of skin to permit further growth and a new layer of skin emerges. This usually occurs two-four times per year, although younger snakes, due to higher growth rates, generally shed their skin more often. Their old skin is simply no longer a good fit. And neither are some of my prior roles. As it is for snakes, shedding is a good thing for me. It lets me acquire and do new things, and provides space for continued growth in the years ahead. I'm not done yet.

HARBINGERS

SILVER ALERT

There they were, at least seven people in wheelchairs who appeared to be in their 60s-80s, queued up and waiting for the boarding call for the flight to Fort Lauderdale. My husband and I were waiting for this flight too; we traveled to Florida two-three times yearly to visit family. As I smiled at this line-up, I suddenly realized that the people in this line could represent a harbinger of my future. I'm sure many of them had plans for retirement, and these plans did not include needing a wheelchair.

"That will never be me," I said to myself. I am in good health and have activities that engage me, and I somehow expect that this will continue indefinitely. But can I be sure?

After we picked up our rental car and were driving on the interstate highway to our condo in Pompano Beach, I noticed the large sign hanging across the highway that declared a "Silver Alert," listing the model of a car and its license plate number. I was familiar with the "Amber Alert" signs in New York, asking drivers to be on the watch for a car that may have a kidnapped child, but I had never seen a "Silver Alert." I imagined that it was for the elderly and sure enough, after Googling it on my iPhone, I learned that it was to alert drivers to a missing senior who may be driving and had some form of dementia. I began searching for the license plate number.

"That will never be me," I said to myself again. I had recently stopped driving, having little use for it in New York City, and rely on my husband to drive when we go to Florida. But the sign did get my attention and reminded me that there may be a time when he may need to give up driving too. I have already noticed that he doesn't see as well at night as he used to. On another recent trip to Florida, as we drove home after a late dinner, he needed to make a turn in an unfamiliar road and we found ourselves up on the curb in the grass. Although poor lighting may have contributed to this, we both knew that his night vision was likely on the decline. What's to be done about these "silver alerts," these reminders that changes may be in store as we age? Not much, other than taking good care of ourselves, adapting to our changing bodies, and paying more attention to our surroundings. Also, making practical adaptations can be helpful, like when in Florida, using Uber-type services for evening trips, and taking advantage of the daylight Early Bird Specials.

MICROAGGRESSIONS FOR SENIORS

"How can I help you, young lady?" the salesman asked me. As you know, dear reader, I am lots of things—retired, sometimes funny, a list-maker, etc.,—but I am not a young lady. I certainly don't want to be addressed as an "old lady," but perhaps "Madam" or just "how can I help you?" would do.

The term "microaggression" refers to a brief, common, often unintended negative or derogatory slight, either verbal or behavioral. The user may actually be well-meaning, but unaware of the negative impact of their statement or behavior. The term was developed by Chester M. Pierce and has been elaborated by Derald Wing Sue. It is generally used to apply to marginalized groups, such as minorities or the disabled, but I have become aware of several types of micro-aggressions experienced by older people, including me:

1. I was in a restaurant with my husband and as we got up to leave a patron said to us, "You are such a cute couple." I think we are a nice couple, usually well-dressed, often friendly to others, but I don't think of us as "cute." This appears to be in the same category as the "young lady" comment I mentioned earlier.

2. The waitress came over to my table to take my lunch order and asked, "What are we having for lunch today?" I'm not sure what she is having for lunch, and I don't intend to share my lunch with anyone. This is a form of infantilization.

3. "How are you, Mama?" or "Do you want this seat, Mama?" These are terms that connote age differences. I have experienced them in stores and on public transportation. I have also heard

the male version, with "Pops" and "Sir" used. I may be old enough to be your mother, and I appreciate that you may be using it as a sign of respect, but I am not your Mama.

4. I have heard a salesperson address an older monolingual Spanish speaker in a louder or slower voice, rather than simply looking for someone who may be able to translate. Don't assume that an older person can't hear you, please; it may be that they simply don't speak your language.

5. Ignoring the older person when someone else is present is also a microaggression. I experienced this when I took my elderly mother for a doctor's visit. The doctor spoke to me about her test results as though my mother wasn't even present. I'm not sure if the doctor felt she couldn't understand, couldn't hear, or wasn't responsible for her own care, but none of these were true. Doing this just made her feel ignored.

So, what's to be done? Identifying micro-aggressions is an important first step in addressing them and reducing their impact. I think that sensitivity to this should be incorporated in the training of professions with substantial public contact, like healthcare workers. In terms of what we can do as individuals, and what I do, I find that if I feel offended, at the minimum, I tell myself that the remark was insensitive even if well-intended. If ongoing contact is anticipated, or if it helps me feel better, then I will say something. In the case of my mother's doctor, I asked him to address her with his comments, and he quickly turned to speak to her directly.

Unassisted Living

On a recent visit to Florida, I called an elderly cousin and learned that her telephone number had been disconnected. Fearing the worst, my husband and I drove to her housing development, where she lived with her spouse, and learned that they had sold their home and moved into a senior facility. Checking the location of their new address, I saw that this facility had three levels: independent living, assisted living, and memory care. I was happy to learn that they were in the "independent living" section, but felt saddened knowing that there was only one direction they could go, and once one starts moving, there's not likely to be any reversal of direction. We didn't get to see them, as my cousin's husband recently had surgery, but we plan to see them on our next trip; hopefully they will still be "independent."

In the past, the term "assisted living" appealed to me, as I appreciated the many ways I was helped by others. For example, I pay someone to clean my house, and my husband does our food shopping and most of the cooking. I wish I had someone to do other errands like buying gifts and picking up items in the pharmacy, so I have wanted more assistance. But when I read the brochures and websites about assisted living facilities, I learned that "assisted living" means something else, not the services I had in mind. The ADLs, or Activities of Daily Living, that generally qualify someone for assisted living status, means that they require assistance for such activities as eating, bathing and toileting, and thank you, but I don't need or want assistance with any of those, not ever, if possible.

So, what's to be done? I plan to continue my independent, relatively unassisted, at home, living status as long as possible. As I am fortunate to be able to afford long-term care insurance for my husband and myself, we will have financial assistance to maintain this status. I don't mind paying for this expensive insurance, as I have a dear friend who is disabled and has been using his long-term care insurance for many years. I think of these payments as my participation in a benevolent Ponzi scheme: money is taken from some to use for others. I don't mind helping him, and I certainly don't mind if I never have to use this insurance for myself or my husband. And, at least for now, an unassisted living status is my preference.

MY FIRST WALKER

I recently had to use a walker for a short time after two benign tumors were removed from my thigh. Muscles were affected during the surgery and when I left the hospital, I was given a walker as a temporary safety measure. It was the basic no-frills type, with two wheels in the front, used by holding on to the side bars and pushing it when walking on flat surfaces.

When I was first given the walker, I thought: "This is not for me, it's for old people." However, when encouraged to use it at the hospital, I felt more secure walking with it.

I live in an apartment and found that while I didn't need to use the walker indoors, it was helpful when I went out to do errands.

And I have made some observations:

First, when I passed someone in the street or in a store with a walker, I felt an immediate connection and smiled or nodded at them. Sometimes I got a response. I was pleased when I did, and I think the other person enjoyed it too.

When I went into my local nail salon, I saw a man with a high-end walker. It had a multi-colored cloth-covered seat, with a big pouch for carrying things. Mine was basic, with no accessories. So, my second observation was that even though I had some ambivalence about using my walker, I certainly didn't want an inferior one.

I found that while the walker is intended to glide easily over the ground, this is almost impossible in the uneven, pocked, New York City streets. I had to be careful not to get my wheel stuck in a crevice or hole, with the potential to cause me to flip over the front of the walker, and wind up worse off than before. In various shops that I entered, carpets or rugs also posed a risk. Thus, while a walker can provide some support, vigilance in its use is necessary.

On one outing with my walker, I went to the supermarket, and left the store with two bags hanging from my wrists. A passerby suggested I get some hooks on my walker to make carrying packages easier. I smiled and said, "Thanks, I can manage, and anyway this is just temporary." Final observation: I was eager to tell people (and myself) that my use of a walker was just temporary.

So, what did I learn? A walker is not just a functional accessory, I have feelings about it. Stereotypes about only old folks using walkers are false; they can be helpful in many circumstances. But I have to remind myself about this, as I have this stereotype internalized, and expect that others do too. I also learned that it felt good to reach out to others using walkers. It helped me form a reassuring bond, however fleeting. It's sort of like acknowledging other dog walkers when you are with your pet, or honking at someone who is driving the same car.

Next, while this first short-term walker may be the only one I will ever have, at some point I may need one for an extended time period. And if I do, dear reader, you can be sure I will get all the upgrades and accessories available, including a fancy comfortable seat and compartments for carrying things. If it helps me get to where I want to go, I will be thankful. And I may even ask my friend the decorator to help me set it up, so I won't have to experience any walker envy.

IT'S OKAY TO ASK FOR HELP

Priding myself on being independent for many years, it has been hard to ask for assistance since I retired. When I was working, I had multiple resources to call on—an administrative assistant, an IT department, a human resources department, and others. All were happy to help in a variety of tasks: to make copies, order lunch, fix my computer, or recruit someone for a new position in my projects. I remember the strong sense of support I felt from my administrative assistant, Carmen, who worked with me for about 20 years. We were once at a large meeting and as we went around the table introducing ourselves, we were asked to describe what we did. When it got to Carmen, her response was, "My job is to do anything that Sherry needs me to do." How fortunate I was! How I miss that support!

And I've had to learn how to find it elsewhere.

I have a contract with Best Buy's Geek Squad, for example. The Squad provides technical assistance for electronics problems. I call them periodically for help with my desktop computer and printer. I feel frustrated that I require specific step-by-step instructions about what to do, but I know I need help. On a recent call I followed a series of instructions to fix my computer which included removing and reattaching wires to the router as well as doing some things on the keyboard. I thought that if they asked me to stand on one leg, stick a finger toward the ceiling, and whisper a magical phrase, I would probably follow all those instructions, since I have no conception of how these things get fixed.

At times, after calling this service for help with a problem, I have had to turn over control of my computer to a Geek squad member. Seeing my cursor move on my screen without my control still seems pretty weird, as though my computer was haunted by an independent being. I thought that if I could turn control of myself over to this being, and it was benevolent, it could make it easier for me to diet and to exercise regularly.

As I get older, I also need help for some mundane tasks around the house. I have become more hesitant about doing some things I used to readily do. When I don't feel like cooking, there are many options for food delivery. If I have a heavy package delivered to my lobby mail room, I will ask the porters who work in my building to bring it to my apartment. And I no longer want to climb ladders, so when things need to be stored at the top of a closet or cabinet that I can't reach, I ask a taller friend or younger family member to do it. I have decided that while I seek to reach new heights in retirement, they won't be ones that put me physically at risk!

So how do I feel about this? I am coming to peace with the idea that it's okay to ask for help as the alternative is even more disturbing; it would mean that my activities would be limited. And I expect that my need to ask for assistance will only increase in the future. I no longer see this as a sign of weakness, and it's helpful to my ego to know that there are areas of expertise I have that others often call on. Perhaps, even more importantly, I find that if I maintain a sense of humor about it all, I can more readily move from frustration about not being able to do something myself to taking action to meet my needs.

FOR THE DURATION

Sometime in her 50s, my mother started using the expression "for the duration." She used it when referring to something that she purchased that she anticipated would last the rest of her life, like a piece of furniture. It helped her justify the cost, as she would never need a replacement. It made me smile when she said it, because we all knew that she only said "for the duration" to allay her discomfort in buying something expensive. But I never expected that the duration would end.

I first started using the term in my 60s, when I needed some expensive dental work, including implants. The cost seemed quite high to me, but I readily agreed to the procedures once I realized that they would be "for the duration."

I have been thinking about this phrase even more since retiring from my full-time work. Not anticipating any more major life changes— like career changes or household moves—I sense I am now living in "the duration" for me.

Not to be somber, but at the very end of her life, my mother lay in a coma for over a year, with a feeding tube going directly into her stomach. This was her final "duration," but unfortunately one in which no more choices could be made.

I have decided to view my "duration" as a time of opportunity. I welcome it as a time in which I can make many choices, including about my surroundings, the activities I do, the people I spend time with, and the places I go.

There are some things that surround me that I hope will continue to be there, like dear friends and family, and good health. And I will no doubt lose some of these. But loss is not the same as discarding what we no longer need.

There is a Yiddish expression that my mother used that I find helpful: *Khap arayn* (kh pronounced with a guttural kh sound). It means "grab it in," or colloquially, "seize the opportunity," or "seize the day." In other words, enjoy the good things in life while you can. I plan to do that for the duration.

SOME GENERAL OBSERVATIONS

THE SENIOR SPECTRUM

After entering senior status, aging is often viewed as a period of increasing declines and disadvantages. However, there are definitely some advantages in moving across the senior spectrum and in going from junior-senior to senior-senior status. Here are some examples:

Someone Offers You a Seat on the Bus:
Junior-Senior: You are insulted!
Senior-Senior: You're grateful and quickly take the seat.

Electronic Devices:
Junior-Senior: You have at least one electronic device you can't get to work, but feel you should keep trying.

Senior-Senior: You have at least three devices you can't get to work, but have someone to call for help.

When You Go to the Gym:
Junior-Senior: Your trainer gives you exercises to help your balance.

Senior-Senior: Folks there are surprised and greet you warmly.

Keeping Engaged in Life:
Junior-Senior: You continue to work and read information in your field.

Senior-Senior: You relax more and read to explore new topics.

Wrinkles and Balding Spots:
Junior-Senior: You notice lines in your face and balding spots on your head, and seek remedies.

Senior-Senior: You no longer notice or care about those changes.

Forgetting Names:

Junior-Senior: You worry about not remembering the names of acquaintances.

Senior-Senior: You call them "dear" and realize some of them don't remember your name, either.

So I will not despair as I traverse the senior spectrum. I look forward to the advantages it can bring.

DIFFERENCES BETWEEN ACTUAL AND FELT AGES

Most older people think of themselves as younger than their age. I am in that group. And I'm also one of those older folks who are surprised when they glimpse themselves in a mirror or glass window: *Who is that person? She couldn't be me—she looks older than I am, and looks like my mother. It must be a mistake.*

So I got to thinking about aging, and the difference between my chronological age and the age I feel I am.

Research has found that many people begin thinking of themselves as younger than their age as early as their 30s, and the perceived difference increases as they get older. I found that in my own family. My 40 year old daughter said she felt like she was in her 30s, and when I asked my 87 year old husband how old he felt, his first response was that he didn't think about it, and then he said he felt like he was in his 50s! And even when I asked how old he thought he looked when he looked in the mirror, he still said he looked in his 50s! How could that be? Is that a gender difference? A visual acuity difference.

Feeling younger than your age is associated with lower rates of depression and better physical health, all good things. There's no real downside to feeling younger than I am, except that it increases my dislike of hearing negative stereotypes about getting older.

Why do I feel younger than my age? Some of the probable contributors are my genetic makeup, having no chronic illnesses, regular exercising (sometimes), staying in touch with family and friends, engaging in activities that stimulate my mind, and watching my diet (sometimes). I also may like feeling younger than my age because in my teenage years I skipped two grades before graduating high school, and for many years I tried acting older than my age to fit in with my peers. I lost some of my young years during that time, and I missed them.

And another reason I feel younger than my age is because I have many things to look forward to, and need years ahead to do them. I recently came across some notes of hopes I had for the next few years. These included seeing my children get the things they wanted. For my daughter (then single) it was to marry and have children; and for my son and his wife, it was to buy their first home. For me, items on the list included retiring and having time to write and explore new cultural activities in New York City. Check, check and check; all these things happened. I feel pleased about them, and fortunate that they have been attained. And I have more to anticipate – to see members of my extended family reach various milestones and other pleasures they seek. And for myself- there are things to see, essays to write, books to read, people I want to spend time with, and perhaps even classes to take to improve my language skills in Spanish and Yiddish. Making plans and anticipating these pleasures helps keep me feeling younger than my age.

Enjoying the present also helps. A neighbor who is 93 told me that she had bought a costly jacket that she liked and then returned it, thinking that buying something so expensive and conspicuous at her age was somehow not right. A short while later she got a gift certificate for the same store, went and saw that the same jacket was there, and she bought it!. Why not buy it at 93? she rhetorically asked, with pleasure and triumph in her voice. Why not indeed! An upside to aging is the realization that we shouldn't defer or deny pleasures for ourselves.

And I find that age differences with others matter less as I get older, broadening my potential friendship network. For example, children who are seven years apart in age, like five and twelve, are not likely to have much in common, and unlikely to become friends. But when you get older, and meet someone with whom you have a seven-year difference in age—like 71 and 78—the age difference itself is meaningless if there are common interests, shared values, and an ease in connecting. A close, even life-long loving friendship can be formed.

At some point in our lives we go through all the age markers for life's milestones. In youth, we look forward to reaching the legal ages to get a driver's license, vote, and buy alcohol. The next legal age marker is not until we are ready to receive social security benefits. As we age, if we have the means, we don't need to feel we are too old to go on that trip, learn a new language, or buy that expensive jacket. And it appears, from recent research into aging, that planning and doing those things that interest us will not only give us pleasure, but will extend the time we have in which to enjoy them. Feeling younger than your age can hold many benefits.

LIVING WITH CONTRADICTORY BELIEFS

I have always liked the concept of cognitive dissonance, developed by psychologist Leon Festinger. I found many examples of it in my life. It occurs when we have two beliefs and behaviors that are contradictory to each other, and we feel uncomfortable because it is difficult to hold on to both of them. We may have to change one of the beliefs or behaviors to reduce our discomfort.

As I get older I am aware of having more contradictory beliefs, but they don't bother me as much. Here are some examples, and how I resolved, or didn't, the contradictions I felt.

Did I make the right decision about selling my condo? Some contradictory feelings arose when I decided to sell my condo in Florida. As I mentioned earlier, we weren't using it very much, it needed repairs, and maintenance and tax costs kept rising. I wanted one less thing to think about taking care of, and the decision seemed easy: I found a go-getter realtor and my family helped me plan how to dispose of the contents. The realtor did some research, came up with what seemed a reasonable price, hired a painter to freshen up the condo, and put the listing on the market. The path seemed clear. But when I met with the realtor in the condo to finalize our arrangements, suddenly it seemed especially lovely to sit on the porch overlooking the pool and golf course. I remembered the peaceful times spent there. Here comes the dissonance: Did I really want to sell it? The answer was yes — for all the reasons I mentioned above. And the condo sold in one day, at the asking price! More dissonance there: I was glad to get a buyer so soon but was the price too low? And since it sold so quickly, does that mean it is really more desirable than I thought? Did I make a mistake and should I have kept it? Will I later regret having sold it?

Some time has now passed. The money I received for selling the condo has been used for family purposes, the objects I cared about that were in the condo were either kept by me or given to family members. I still go to Florida and now stay with family when I visit, and no regrets. The dissonance was only temporary.

Why don't I fully adhere to healthy living behaviors? I am aware of the recommendations for healthy living and know I should diet to lose weight, drink alcohol infrequently, and never smoke. These recommendations are science-based and I believe they will improve my health. But here's the dissonance: I enjoy food and often eat out with friends, alcohol at dinner enhances the meal and contributes to my relaxation, and sometimes I still crave smoking cigarettes. I am dealing with these contradictions, with mixed success. I have "yo-yo" eating habits – at parties or family celebrations I eat some things that can contribute to weight gain, and deal with this by cutting back on subsequent days. Sometimes that works. In terms of alcohol— that seems to be resolving itself—I am finding that if I have more than one drink, I don't feel well later that evening, so I have been reducing my intake. As for smoking, although I was a pack-a-day smoker starting in my teens and stopped after about 20 years, I sometimes still crave it, especially when I am with smokers. So I "bum" cigarettes when I am with people who smoke; fortunately there aren't too many of these anymore. I have mixed results in resolving these dissonant behaviors and beliefs regarding healthy living, but hey, I'm human, and all our contradictions are not easily nor fully resolvable. I am OK with the resolutions I have reached.

Am I getting too old to do some things? I feel energetic and eager to do and explore many things. But I grew up with a family, and at a time, when reaching your 50s, or retiring, generally meant you couldn't do much anymore. What I saw in my relatives and family friends who had reached this stage was that visiting family, watching TV and eating were the major activities. I think for some of them, more active engagement in life was seen as too costly, or potentially even harmful. Cardiac problems and deaths were not infrequent, especially among middle-aged men.

But I believe times have changed, and medical treatments have advanced, so we are healthier and living longer. Also, my family's views about staying close to home were influenced in part by their origins; they were Jews who came from Eastern Europe in the 1920s, at a time when their surroundings held antisemitism and other potential dangers for them.

Here's the dissonance: can I continue my exploration of new experiences or should I cut back on my activities? Is it safer to stay closer to home, and only engage in what I have been doing, since I know I have been safe that way? *Lign Ayngeleygt* is a Yiddish expression my mother used, as an admonition to "lay quiet, stay where you are." Perhaps that was functional for her and her peers, but I have learned that my beliefs and behaviors can be different from what I saw when I was young, and

I can readily adhere to another Yiddish expression, *l'chaim,* or "to life", which I see as an encouragement to enjoy all life has to offer.

So, while life may continue to present experiences and moments that elicit contradictory or dissonant beliefs and behaviors, resolutions are available—and if not, we can learn to live with them in peace. No dissonance about that!

IN CONCLUSION

ACT YOUR AGE

As a child, I remember parents and others telling me to "act my age," usually when they thought my behavior seemed immature, sometimes when they felt I was reaching too far beyond what was appropriate for my age. But what does it mean to "act my age" as an older, retired person. Should I reflect on my accomplishments, provide wisdom to youth, and otherwise rest, as some believe?

During a recent Thanksgiving holiday, my husband and I took two of our grandchildren out for brunch the day after the big feast. It gave us an opportunity to talk with them and to hear how they are doing without lots of friends and family around.

We had a great time talking together. They are bright, talented young adults, both in college, and we were eager to hear about their classes, their college social life, and their plans for the future.

They shared their thoughts and ideas with us, and we were supportive, complimentary, and asked many questions.

They asked about us as well and we mainly provided updates about minor health issues and future travel plans. I think we focused on these because we believed these were the topics they anticipated we would talk about.

But as I listened to them I felt a strange stirring in my emotions, a feeling that at this point in my life I was not that different from them. I too have aspirations and enthusiasm for my future. These plans don't involve developing a life-long career plan nor finding a partner, thankfully, but they seem exciting to me, and I no longer feel the pressure of having to make the "right" decisions. I am taking Spanish classes to improve my conversational Spanish, and hope to get good enough to do volunteer work with Hispanic immigrants. I also started a blog that helps me express and find humor in this stage of life, and I enjoy sharing my thoughts with others. There are also places I want to explore and books I want to read that I never had time for before. And I look forward to making plans for new activities and explorations.

Some psychosocial theorists call my stage of life late adulthood, usually considered to start at age 65. I am fortunate in being healthy and financially stable, and for the most part, I can choose how I wish to spend my time. As I started to think about the time ahead, I looked into what has been written about this stage of life to see how it applies to me, and perhaps find some guidance. One of the early theoreticians who wrote about late adulthood was Erik Erikson, who described late adulthood as the final stage of life, from age 65 to death. He described this as a period of looking back on one's accomplishments and either feeling satisfied or disappointed, or as he called it, developing a sense of integrity or despair. I do some of that looking back, but I find I am more interested in looking forward to what I hope to do in the future. Some may say I have not yet learned to "act my age," but that's fine with me. I believe that as it is *my* age, I want to fully own what I do with it. I'm not done yet.

ACKNOWLEDGEMENTS

Several people helped in the development of this work. Carol Bergman, the mentor of my writing workshop, and all the workshop members, including Ed Koenig, Eric Stotter, Jenny Griffin, and Betty Leigh Hutcheson, were supportive and encouraged my efforts; Carol edited all the essays. My husband, Douglas Lipton, encouraged me in developing my blog, and I also thank my readers, who sent me comments that helped me realize they also experienced many of the things I wrote about. This motivated me to create this anthology. Foremost among my readers and supporters was Susan Tross, who commented on the first versions of many of these pieces. To them all I send my gratitude.

(Photo by Juliana Suárez-Lipton)

SHERRY DEREN

BIOGRAPHY

Sherry Deren was trained as a social psychologist and spent most of her career conducting and directing federally funded behavioral research studies related to drug use and HIV. After retiring from NYU as a Founding Center Director and a Visiting Research Professor, she began a blog to express some of her thoughts and experiences related to aging: humorandaging.com. She has been enjoying the many cultural and other benefits of NYC and exploring the freedom and choices that retirement makes possible. She lives in Manhattan with her husband, is a devoted mother and grand-mother, and has a large extended family.

www.ingramcontent.com/pod-product-compliance
Lightning Source LLC
Chambersburg PA
CBHW060519130626
46553CB00002B/559